Making difficult decisions

MAKING DIFFICULT DECISIONS

How to be decisive and get the business done

Peter Shaw CB

CAPSTONE

First published in 2008
Capstone Publishing Ltd. (a Wiley Company)
The Atrium, Southern Gate, Chichester, PO19 8SQ, UK.
www.wileyeurope.com
Email (for orders and customer service enquires): cs-books@wiley.co.uk

Other Wiley Editorial Offices
John Wiley & Sons Inc., 111 River Street, Hoboken, NJ 07030, USA
Jossey-Bass, 989 Market Street, San Francisco, CA 94103–1741, USA
Wiley-VCH Verlag GmbH, Boschstr. 12, D-69469 Weinheim, Germany
John Wiley & Sons Australia Ltd, 42 McDougall Street, Milton, Queensland 4064,
Australia
John Wiley & Sons (Asia) Pte Ltd, 2 Clementi Loop #02–01, Jin Xing Distripark, Singapore
129809
John Wiley & Sons Canada Ltd, 22 Worcester Road, Etobicoke, Ontario, Canada M9W 1L1
Wiley also publishes its books in a variety of electronic formats. Some content that appears
in print may not be available in electronic books.

A catalogue record for this book is available from the British Library and the Library of
Congress.

ISBN 978–1-84112–742–2

Typeset in Photina by Sparks, Oxford – www.sparkspublishing.com
Printed and bound in Great Britain by TJ International Ltd, Padstow, Cornwall

Substantial discounts on bulk quantities of Capstone Books are available to corporations,
professional associations and other organisations. For details telephone John Wiley & Sons on
(+44) 1243 770441, fax (+44) 1243 770571 or email corporatedevelopment@wiley.co.uk

Dedicated to our son Colin
who is an inspiration as he makes difficult decisions well

Contents

Acknowledgements

Many people have shaped my thinking in writing this book. Some have influenced directly as a result of detailed conversation while the influence of others has been less overt. I am grateful to them all.

Many people have given generously of their time. I have sought the perspective of a wide range of people. The following have been especially generous with their time: Nicky Munro, John Thomas, Chris Banks, Stephen Timms, Charles Macrae, Pete Worrall, William Patey, Norman Haste, Philip Wood, Peter Collis, James Hirst, Jane Willis, John Suffolk, John Gieve, Justin McCracken, Linda Freestone, Archie Hughes, Martin Oakley, Gill Lucas, Paul Connew, Leigh Lewis, David Normington, Julie Taylor, Eoin McLennon-Murray, Alice Perkins, Nick Holgate, Paul Buckley, Mel Zuydam, Suma Chakrabarti, Finlay Scott, Julian Duxfield, Anna Ford, John Saunders, Dorcas Batstone, Gordon Wetherell, Bill Brackenridge, Roger King, Paul West, Jeremy Cooke, Lesley Strathie, Charlie Massey, May O'Keefe, Robert Green, Adele Townsend, Peter Buckley, Jane Frost, Nicola Haskins, Andrew Holmes, Una O'Brien, Sunil Patel, Andrew Jackson and Mal Singh. I take full responsibility for the views in the book but the perspective of those mentioned above has been invaluable. These special people come from very diverse worlds: they have all been perceptive sources of wisdom.

I am grateful to a number of people who read the manuscript and provided excellent feedback. The comments of Mairi Eastwood, Robin Linnecar, Heather Dawson, and Hilary Douglas helped clarify the thinking and meant that the text is clearer than it might have been!

My coaching clients have been a tremendous source of wisdom. I thoroughly enjoy working with them as they reflect on difficult decisions they have to take. Often we go on a journey of exploration together talking through the implications of different options. I hope that in some small way the conversations have helped my clients reach a point of clarity on their own next steps.

I am grateful to Nick Macpherson for contributing a foreword to the book. I always admired his clarity of thinking when we worked in the same areas and have observed with great pleasure the thoughtful leadership he brings as a Permanent Secretary.

John Wiley have been a very supportive publisher. Sally Smith commissioned the book, John Moseley has taken it through to the near final text and Jenny Ng has looked after the detailed arrangements for publication.

My Executive Assistant, Claire Pratt, has managed the diary carefully to ensure that I have been able to talk to a wide range of people in preparing the book. Judy Smith has typed the manuscript with great skill and continuous good humour. Claire and Judy have been a brilliant support team throughout the process of writing a number of books in the last four years.

I am grateful to my colleagues at Praesta Partners who are always a source of excellent wisdom and advice. As a team of coaches from a range of different backgrounds there is a continuous sharing of ideas and approaches where we are able to learn from each other.

It has been good to work with colleagues as fellow members of Godalming College Governing Body and St. John's College Governing Body in Durham. Together we have had to take hard decisions and welcomed the mutual support and challenge from colleagues. Taking difficult decisions together has been much more rewarding than doing it separately.

I have refined the ideas in the book in a number of seminars with diverse groups including high potential staff in the UK Health and Safety Executive, curates in the diocese of Derby, a senior learning set at the UK Food Standards Agency, senior leaders on the UK Cabinet Office Pathways programme and a Men's Breakfast at St. Paul's Church, Tervuren in Brussels.

I am grateful to my family who have encouraged me in the writing and allowed me the opportunity to retreat into the study with dictaphone in hand. I am no expert in decision-making. I acknowledge in particular the influence of those who have helped me crystallise my own thinking when I needed to make decisions. Colin, to whom this book is dedicated, has always been an astute decision maker. I admire his ability to make quick decisions when playing sport at international level. As parents we must have done something right!

Finally I believe that decision-making is about drawing from our intellectual, physical, emotional and spiritual awareness. At the heart of good decision-making is being open-minded and yet rooted in your own values at the same time. It is that combination of determination and reflection, of focus alongside flexibility, that helps ensure we make the best possible decisions.

Other books by Peter Shaw

Mirroring Jesus as Leader, Grove, 2004

Conversation Matters: how to engage effectively with one another, Continuum, 2005

The Four Vs of Leadership: vision, values, value-added, vitality, Capstone, 2006

Finding Your Future: the second time around, Darton, Longman and Todd, 2006

Business Coaching: achieving practical results through effective engagement, Capstone, 2007. (Co-authored with Robin Linnecar)

Forthcoming books

The Christian Leader in the Secular World of Work, Authentic, 2010.

The author's royalties are going to Tearfund,
which provides practical help for those in poverty
to enable them to have a future and make their own decisions.

Foreword

I first met Peter Shaw more than twenty years ago. I had just joined the Treasury, and my job was to provide economic advice to the labour market policy team which Peter was then leading. The Treasury of those days attached a slightly lower priority to good management than it does now. And the building in Great George Street – consisting then of austere monkish cells – was less conducive to good communications than its modern open plan successor. To me, at that time, Peter shone out like a beacon. In a world of hard-nosed introverts, here was a man of rare compassion and humanity who could communicate and lead. To the civil service's credit, these skills were recognised, and all too rapidly he returned to his home department on promotion. Our paths have continued to cross over the years, more recently in his second career as a leadership coach, and it is a great privilege to be asked to write the Foreword to this book.

In any day, we all make hundreds of decisions. Most are easy. Some are difficult. It is the latter on which we tend to need help. Peter's insight is to take the mystique out of the decision-making process; the faddish jargon of the traditional self-help book is not for him. He encourages us to deconstruct the components of a good decision through the simple paradigm of the 4Cs – clarity, conviction, courage and communication – and then goes on to provide some essential building blocks to develop our capabilities further.

Peter's analysis resonates for me working in the Treasury, where a dominant theme is the allocation of scarce resources. The Treasury is a small institution, whose walls always seem to be about to be breached by the marauding hoards of spending departments and their demands. (Of course, from a spending department perspective, life seems very different!) This places a high premium on achieving 'clarity': the key elements, set out by Peter in Chapter 2 are music to a Treasury official's ears: objectivity, defining the problem, being clear on the context, ensuring sound analysis, and so on.

But in my experience it is the less cerebral side to decision-making, the subject of Peter's later chapters, which is critical if decisions are really going to stand the test of time. This is about recognising the human factor.

First, in relation to those affected. As David Normington is quoted as saying in Chapter 3: 'most of the decisions that are troublesome are all about people in the end'. Understanding how others will react by putting yourself in their shoes is a start. Investing in team building can also yield dividends. Using psychometrics has made the Treasury Management Board more effective: I have a better understanding of how my colleagues will react to decisions, ideas and events, and they have a better understanding of how I will react. That has been really useful in resolving difficult issues like the implementation of a challenging spending review settlement.

Secondly, it's about nurturing your own decision-making space. That's partly about time – sleeping on a decision can make all the difference (Chapter 13 on 'dealing with your hopes and fears' is relevant here). It is also literally about physical space – a walk round St James' Park or a trip to a café. It is about being able to step back and remain calm, when all the pressure is to immerse yourself in the adrenalin of the moment. Good support systems are critical, whether in a domestic or work environment.

I was struck by Peter's section on the 'importance of conversations with colleagues'. In any job, you develop certain key relationships which provide real emotional and intellectual sustenance – I have a colleague with a very different personality type from me: I always find discussing any difficult decision with him reenergising, and he assures me that the relationship is reciprocal.

Peter's book covers all these issues and more. And I commend it to anybody who is facing difficult and demanding decisions.

Nicholas Macpherson, Permanent Secretary, H M Treasury

Introduction

'The die is cast' were the words of Julius Caesar when he crossed the Rubicon. This was only a small stream forming part of the boundary between Italy and Gaul but the crossing of it marked the beginning of the war with Pompey. A decision had been taken with consequences both known and unknown. Crossing the Rubicon was just going across a river, but it was also a decision from which there was no turning back.

'Decisions, decisions. Why so many decisions!' protested the 18-year-old when there were so many choices about which university, which course, whether to have a gap year, which friends to spend time with, which summer job to do and (unspoken) what to do about those parents! Taking decisions at age 18 is a shock to the system, but is just the start of a long process of making choices.

How good are we at making decisions? Sometimes the decisions flow naturally. The correct choice is so obvious. At other times we vacillate, procrastinate and hesitate. There is an exterior of confidence and a chasm of doubt inside. We project an appearance of weighing up of the options, while in our darker moments we wrestle with uncertainty and bemoan our lack of clarity.

Sometimes our way of handling difficult decisions is to hold on to a rigid view with a tight grip, letting our prejudices determine our actions. On other occasions we have no grip at all and enjoy floundering in our own indecision. Being a victim of indecision can be such a wonderful indulgence sometimes.

What makes the difference between times when the decision is relatively easy and others where we flounder? How can we school ourselves to take difficult decisions well and calmly without the intellectual or emotional wrestling or even agony that sometimes comes with difficult decisions? Is there some way we can make a step change in our capability to make difficult decisions well?

What is a difficult decision? It may be about policy or operational choices, the management of people, the commitment of financial resources or the time committed to different activities. It might be about the balance between short-term and long-term consequences. It could be decisions that affect nobody other than ourselves or decisions which influence a wide range of different people.

Sometimes our decisions have no consequences other than for today. Sometimes the decisions which we think are just about today have consequences over a long period. When the Iroquois made a decision, they said, 'How does it affect seven generations in the future?' They were steeped in history and recognised that decisions taken today had outcomes for many years ahead.

Principles of decision-making

Whatever the nature of the decision you or your organisation is taking, the principles of good decision-making are the same. It is all about:

- **clarity**: utter objectivity about the issue, the context and the consequences;
- **conviction**: the place of intuition, values and trained judgement;
- **courage**: turning belief into action to build next steps;
- **communication**: embracing listening, engaging and persuading.

The heart of good decision-making is balancing clarity and conviction. It is the interplay between analysis and beliefs, logical thinking and the 'gut' reaction that is at the heart of how we make decisions. Courage and communication are then essential elements in being decisive, taking forward difficult decisions effectively and getting the business done.

Our ability to make decisions depends on our own self-understanding and how we handle ourselves when making decisions. We need to know when we are good at making decisions and when we are in danger of being less effective because of blinkering, avoidance, vulnerability or even fear. Understanding our own strengths and weaknesses is essential to our being able to improve our ability to make good decisions and move on. Understanding the way other people make decisions provides an important input, especially those people whose styles and preferences are very different to our own.

These four elements of clarity, conviction, courage and communication apply just as readily to strategic or short-term decisions, to work or personal choices and to addressing life choices about our use of time and energy. Developing the capability to make decisions well in one area of our lives can enhance our ability to make decisions in other areas of our lives. For example the way we make decisions on the sports field can directly affect our ability to make decisions in the work place.

The aim of this book is to enable the reader to:

- clarify their own thinking about the best way of making difficult decisions;
- view the decision-making of others in a more aware and accurate way so that there is greater understanding of why others reach the decisions they do;
- understand their own preferences and foibles in making difficult decisions;
- be able to take difficult decisions with greater confidence, less personal anguish and worry.

The successful decision maker needs enough self-awareness to see themselves as others see them, to acknowledge their mistakes and not to take themselves too seriously while being fully committed to the decisions they are taking.

The book draws on the experiences of a wide range of people in leadership positions covering both the private, public and voluntary sectors. It covers the perspectives of senior leaders wrestling with financial investment decisions, Permanent Secretaries leading major UK government departments and those with difficult decisions in the justice world including judges, a prison governor and a Chief Constable. It includes senior leaders in educational establishments and hospitals making decisions that affect the long-term future and well being of individuals. It draws on examples of decision-making in the sports world. The examples deliberately come from people of varying degrees of seniority. The issues facing a junior supermarket manager and a government minister may be very different in scale, but will often contain similar dilemmas about facts and feelings with similar time pressures to make quick decisions.

The 4 Cs of clarity, conviction, courage and communication have resonated with leaders facing difficult decisions in a wide range of different sectors including politics, government, financial institutions, education establishments, hospitals, prisons, manufacturing firms and retail organisations. These all are very different spheres but they all require decisions to be made thoughtfully, decisively and often quickly. Finding the balance between clarity and conviction has resonated with every leader I have spoken to as being what good decision-making is all about.

How to use this book

The book can be read from start to finish or used as a resource to address particular issues.

Part 1 of the book addresses the 4 Cs of making difficult decisions. It includes a particular focus on the balance between clarity and conviction where various leaders from different spheres talk thoughtfully about how they have tried to ensure they get that balance right and what they have learnt when they got it wrong.

Part 2 looks at taking forward key aspects of making difficult decisions addressing:

- **applying the learning from good decision makers:** which looks at the experience of role models in decision-making;
- **embedding the ability to make difficult decisions**: which is about learning effectively from our experience;
- **enabling others to make difficult decisions**: which is about enabling individuals and teams to have the courage, confidence and resources to make choices effectively;
- **key questions in making difficult decisions**: if we are able to ask the right questions it helps making difficult decisions more manageable.

Part 3 addresses making difficult decisions in particular circumstances. It sets out practical steps which aim to provide a stimulus for deciding what action to take. It considers the following areas:

- **making difficult decisions as the boss:** this includes introducing better decision-making into your senior team, changing the values of your organisation, taking a decision when your senior team have differing views, moving senior members out of your team and being compelled to readdress an issue;
- **making difficult decisions in relation to your boss:** this covers enabling your boss to face up to a decision they are ducking, influencing your boss to make a decision in support of your favoured approach, holding firm when your boss is demanding an immediate decision, and rebuilding a relationship after a difference of view on a decision;
- **making difficult decisions in relation to your peers:** this includes persuading a peer that the decision they are moving towards is wrong,

building support from colleagues for a decision you want to take, building a wider network which will enable decisions to be made more effectively in the future, and building a relationship with peers which provides a framework for future decision-making;

- **dealing with your hopes and fears:** this includes handling a situation where you are indecisive, facing a decision you do not like taking, recovering from a wrong decision, and holding firm when courage fails you;
- **addressing values and priorities:** this includes guarding against difficult decisions sapping energy, coping when work and personal priorities are at odds with each other, or work and personal values are at odds with each other, and the balancing of long- and short-term personal priorities.

Your reflections on decision-making

My hope for you is that reflecting on these elements of **clarity**, **conviction**, **courage** and **communication** will give you the stimulus to be bolder in your decision-making while being rooted in your own values. I hope it will help you move to another place when making choices, which brings together your rational capabilities, your emotional awareness and your personal values and priorities. If you are able to make just one choice better, then it will have been worth your investment of time reflecting on clarity, conviction, courage and communication.

My hope is that you will get into a rhythm which works for you in making decisions. Some decisions you will take semi-automatically while others will involve careful thought and discussion. Some will need to be taken in five minutes while others might take months.

The best leaders do not get it right all the time. Great leaders look back and learn from their mistakes. They avoid a long-term sense of failure and attach no stigma to learning through failure. They sit it out without destroying themselves with self-blame. They learn from decisions with small consequences and then test out decisions on a wider platform. The best of leaders learn to wait. There is a right timing for decisions. Sometimes it is best to wait for time to pass and attitudes to change. Sometimes that can be an excuse for inaction. The skill is getting this balance right.

Decision-making should not always be easy or straightforward. If it is, there may be something missing. Continually testing your decision-making against the facts, your intuition, your values and the perspective of colleagues, customers and critics is a tough but necessary step in refining your ability to make difficult decisions.

When you feel uneasy about a decision it may not be because you are a bad decision maker. It may be that you have missed out a key factor. It is worth asking: why do I feel unsettled about a decision? It might be because it is outside your comfort zone, it parallels difficult decisions in the past, another strand needs to be explored, or it is inconsistent with values and principles which are important to you.

Sometimes in our desire to prove ourselves to be able to make decisions we try to make every decision, much to the dismay of our staff and our families. Being good at decision-making is sometimes about letting others make decisions and living happily with the outcome of those decisions.

We can become better incrementally at making difficult decisions through fine tuning our ability to use facts and feelings well, but decision-making should never become too easy if we are to use our gifts of intellectual, emotional, physical and spiritual awareness to the best possible effect. So be ready to enjoy and not be daunted by the decisions you need to take.

Peter Shaw CB, Pall Mall, London, January 2008

Part 1

The 4Cs of making difficult decisions

This section of the book covers the four key strands of clarity, conviction, courage and communication and illustrates a set of practical steps in respect of each theme.

These themes cover:

- **clarity:** ensuring objectivity about the issue, the context and the circumstances;
- **conviction:** bringing intuition, values and trained judgement;
- **courage:** turning belief into action to build next steps;
- **communication:** continually listening, engaging and persuading.

It looks at the interrelationship between clarity and conviction drawing from the experience of leaders in a wide variety of contexts suggesting an approach to balancing these different dimensions and then looks in turn at each theme.

In working through the 4Cs questions might be:

- Do the 4Cs ring true for me?
- How good am I at getting the balance right between clarity and conviction?
- How do I assess my courage and ability to communicate effectively in taking difficult decisions?
- How do I want to strengthen my capabilities in each area?
- Do I think the 4Cs miss out any crucial areas?

Chapter 1

Balancing clarity and conviction

A t the heart of effective decision-making is balancing clarity and conviction. The natural starting point for different individuals will be at different points on this spectrum. What can we learn from the experience of others in balancing clarity and conviction and how can we develop an approach in ourselves which takes forward the best of both dimensions?

This chapter looks at various perspectives on the balance between clarity and conviction and then sets out an illustrative set of questions to help weigh up the balance between clarity and conviction applicable in a wide range of situations.

The stark reality

How often have you been faced with making a decision on the basis of limited evidence? You are balancing facts and your sense of the right next steps. It could be one of the following scenarios.

- You have a purchasing decision to make. You have weighed up all the evidence but you are uncomfortable about the organisation which comes out top on the factual analysis.
- You have a recruitment decision to make and are confident that one candidate is the best candidate although you cannot be precise about why this person feels so much better than the other candidates.
- You have a decision to make about whether to send a critical e-mail. You feel emotionally that a message needs to be sent. Do you hold back and reassess the facts in the cold light of day before you finally decide whether or not to send the e-mail?
- You have a major strategic decision to make about the use of resources. You have loads of documentation, but you are in danger of not seeing the wood for the trees. Your gut instinct is clear, but is there a risk that you go with your gut instinct when working hard through the analytic data is the right next step.

These decisions are of different orders of magnitude. The recruitment and strategic resourcing decisions will have major long-term consequences. The e-mail may be the cause of short-term angst but with no long-term consequences. Yet in a busy day your mind may be moving from one type of decision to another. Some may seem more difficult than others during the day, while at 4am the relativities might seem very different.

For all of these decisions there is an oscillation between facts and feelings. There are elements of clarity and elements of conviction bouncing up against each other in your brain. So how do you balance clarity and conviction in a wide range of different contexts?

Smart choices

In their book entitled *Smart Choices: A Practical Guide to Making Better Life Decisions*, (Broadway Books, New York, 1999) Hammond, Keeney and Raiffa talk of effective decision-making processes fulfilling six criteria:

- It focuses on what is important;
- It is logical and consistent;
- It acknowledges both subjective and objective factors and blends analytical with intuitive thinking;
- It requires only as much information and analysis as is necessary to resolve a particular dilemma;
- It encourages and guides the gathering of relevant information and informed opinion;
- It is straightforward, reliable, easy to use and flexible.

The authors see addressing these criteria as relevant for decisions that are either major or minor. They suggest eight keys to effective decision-making:

1 Work on the right decision problem.
2 Specify your objectives.
3 Create imaginative alternatives.
4 Understand the consequences.
5 Grapple with your trade-offs.
6 Clarify your uncertainties.
7 Think hard about your risk tolerance.
8 Consider linked decisions.

The authors set out a very rational approach dealing with a range of different practical decisions. Their thrust is on as much objectivity as possible with personal preference only playing a limited part. The difficulty is that sometimes it is not possible to systemise decision-making in the way advocated in the book. But the eight keys above provide a helpful starting point.

Living with reality

This section records the perspective of three leaders from very different worlds about living with reality. Nicky Munroe, a former Director General within the Scottish Executive, talks about coping with decision-making in a situation which is neither orderly nor straightforward and where decisions are messy and only partial information is available. Her perspective is,

> *'The leader has to be increasingly good at coping with ambiguity. The first time a major decision has to be handled which is not straightforward you can feel a bad leader. But everyone is going to hit these hard situations. In a world of ambiguity, leadership is about having to take difficult decisions in difficult situations. It is right to take account of a mix of rational and emotional factors.'*

Sometimes the focus has to be at the clarity end. Lord Justice John Thomas, a senior High Court Judge, talks of being very careful about 'gut feelings'. His perspective is,

> *'Gut feelings are often wrong. You need to think them through very carefully. Setting aside thinking time is important. Never make a decision when cross. I think better under pressure: you need to understand in what circumstances you think in the most effective way. When I have difficult decisions to take I like to talk to people and by articulating things you illustrate what the problem is. Look at the upsides and downsides: what is the downside of taking a particular decision. Always sleep on it: this perspective is a product of seeing lawyers make hasty decisions and then regret it. Work out how you are going to put over a decision: see how it is going to operate practically. You need courage to face your people and explain the difficult decisions. In many cases you may think that they will want to be critical, but if you talk to them they will listen. If you don't face them they will grumble and the issues will get out of proportion.'*

Chris Banks from his perspective as a senior executive in the food and drink industry readily acknowledges that instinct does play a big role. His perspective is people in business are paid to act on their own judgement and to make decisions, he recognises the danger of individuals using data that supports their conclusions. Chris sees the good organisation trying to slow down decision-making to enable managers to ask better questions in order to get below inbuilt prejudices. He sees the merits of decisions by many companies spending time retraining people to reduce their prejudices. His perspective is that,

> *'An important issue is your mental model for decision-making: you need to make quick judgements in many businesses, so you need to be trained so that you are clear what mental model you are using.'*

Balancing clarity and conviction where information is partial

Leaders are always wrestling with situations where information is partial. Looking at a range of examples can give insights into how best individuals balance clarity and conviction. Examples below include a government minister, a Crown Prosecutor, a health and safety inspector, the chief executive of a European business, a UK ambassador, a leader of major infrastructure projects, a hospital surgeon in Africa and the chief executive of a national organisation and a supermarket junior manager. These are live examples of individuals facing and coping with the balance between clarity and conviction.

A government minister

Stephen Timms from his experience as a UK government minister talks of his role in making decisions when he receives detailed advice. He believes it is important to give a clear direction of travel at each stage. Where there are steps he wants to see happen it is his responsibility to tell people so that there is no lack of clarity about the next steps. He says that when he overturns a decision it is often where his gut feeling tells him there is something wrong. His perspective is that turning over a decision should not happen very often because of the importance of giving clear steers in advance. But when he receives recommendations, testing whether they are right involves both clarity of thinking, and also a gut feeling which is based on long experience of the effect of different types of actions.

Stephen tells the story of when he was asked to speak at a rally in support of a family who felt victimised. There was strong local feeling and the organisers were keen that he was there. He felt it was the right decision to accept the invitation but the decision was difficult and not comfortable. The reasons influencing his decision were both intellectual and intuitive. His intuition told him it was a bad idea not to be there: it was far better to be seen to be there and able to express a view. Eighty per cent of the decision was based on gut feeling. He tested this intuitive feeling by asking a number of people for their perspectives including both local people and a ministerial colleague. He felt a strong moral obligation to speak at the rally and took what he believed to be the right decision having checked out his intuitive judgement with some key people.

A Crown Prosecutor

Senior lawyers are in the business of weighing up the facts and then reaching a judgement about what they believe is right based often on conflicting evidence. When the police refer a case to the Crown Prosecution Service the decision to be taken is: does the CPS charge the defendant or not? When the issues are clear there is no problem about taking a decision. Decisions are based on the code of practice for Crown Prosecutors: a decision to prosecute a case has to pass both the evidential test and the public interest test. The options are to decide to charge, to decide there is insufficient evidence or it is not in the public interest to proceed, or to seek further information.

The Crown Prosecutor has to make a decision based on whatever facts they have available. Charles talks of making decisions based on his perspective following the weighing up of evidence. He says,

> *'You will have often seen the scenarios before. You will understand the pattern but you are always conscious that you have to check that you are drawing on wisdom and not prejudice. My experience is that I draw from my own experience and the counsel of others in talking the case through with them and drawing on their experience. You ask the question would a tribunal, properly directed, be more likely to convict than not?'*

Charles says that the steps going on in his mind when he takes a decision include:

- what are the points that strike him from the initial read of the material?
- the quality of the content and the statements;
- the first impressions about the reliability of those involved;
- the relevance of past legal cases;
- reflections from previous similar situations;
- what are the key features of the evidence on which the case hinges?
- what are the potential defences that may be raised at trial?

The danger is that a request for more information triggers further information which is extraneous: if things get delayed it could mean losing the case because witnesses are lost. The test is how often does this further information change the mind of the prosecutor and what is the diminishing return from further information if the time lapse means that a case might not be brought to trial.

Deciding whether or not to prosecute is an interesting example of weighing up evidence when there is limited clarity. The prosecutor inevitably has to apply an intuitive or judgemental test to the evidence and then assess their judgement. Whilst the Crown Prosecutor determines whether there is sufficient evidence to charge a defendant, the ultimate decision as to guilt is a matter for the court.

A health and safety inspector

Health and safety inspectors have to make difficult and controversial decisions about who to prosecute. The perspective of a number of inspectors reflecting on difficult decisions they have been involved in can be summarised as follows:

- We had a decision whether to investigate or not and decided not to do so. The key issue was weighing up gut instincts and facts. We were not convinced and decided not to investigate.
- Sometimes you have a clear feeling for what is fair. The question is how much do you value your gut reaction or do you buy a bit more time asking more questions, but at the end of the day you have to take a decision.
- Sometimes I think I have been taken in by industry. It is important to have a process to check that decisions have been taken effectively. The importance of clarity of feedback is vital, you have to talk to people and know the business and make clear what your level of interest is.

The health and safety inspectors recognise the difficulties inherent in the decisions they take. They have to weigh up the evidence carefully: at the heart of their decisions is who do they trust, what are the likely implications of their decision and what further enlightenment would more investigation provide. At the end of the day they have to make a judgement that they feel comfortable with, drawing on the evidence, their professional experience and their judgement about what is fair. Their belief is that when a group of people taking difficult decisions are wrestling hard with the different variables, those affected by the decisions can have maximum confidence in the outcome of those decisions.

A chief executive of a European business

Pete has held a major chief executive role in a European organisation in the aeronautics world. In terms of balancing clarity and conviction some of his key considerations are,

> *'What is particularly important is clarity about outcomes and risk mitigation. You need to understand where different parties are coming from and what is the maximum contribution they are prepared to make. You often need to try to find different ways round problems.*
>
> *Before making a decision you need to have the right sources of information available. What do people really want out of this exercise? In a negotiation what extra element will give somebody something that means they can accept the whole package? It is not always the logical thing that makes the difference; it might be a trade-off in another area.*
>
> *It is important to have different sources of information so that you see if there are discrepancies. Sometimes making a pact with an opposite number can help in terms of building alliances.*
>
> *Try hard not to alienate colleagues, since you may need their support during the negotiations, but also don't shy away from healthy conflict. Never fight a battle on two fronts at the same time, since you risk being divided and conquered.'*

A UK ambassador

William Patey is a former UK Ambassador in Baghdad. He is not afraid to make decisions and relies 'on judgement with experience with a little bit of detachment'. He starts by wanting to know what the available facts are with clarity of vision important in order to use that information wisely. Key questions then become:

- what do we need to know to make the decision now?
- what do we currently know?

In Baghdad there were frequent decisions to be taken on military action. The professional officers might get operational intelligence in relation to a hostage situation and want to take action. In certain circumstances they would need political authority from the ambassador. In a normal situation the ambassador would consult London, but if time is limited, the ambassador decides. Sometimes William would say 'yes' on the basis of answers to questions like:

- what are the risks to the soldiers?
- what would be the fallout if it went wrong?

He said the soldiers were glad to have an ambassador who was willing to make a decision. He would inform London of the decision and then see their reaction. The response from London was often that they were glad he had taken the decision. His decisions in these circumstances led to no disasters and did lead to the release of at least one key hostage.

William Patey comments that in making these decisions,

> 'I trusted the judgement of people giving me the briefing. They were the people carrying the physical risk. Before they made a recommendation they had considered the risks carefully. I had confidence in their advice and had no need to question their military judgement. In addition I had a lot of background information and knowledge and could make a reasonable assessment of the risks. Key questions in my mind would be, what if it went wrong and what if it went right? It would be balancing the risks against the results. I would have a clear picture in my mind of the consequences of not taking the decision. If you don't decide to agree to an action you are still taking a decision. It may be easier to make the decision 'no' but in these situations you cannot avoid a decision.'

William was very conscious that when he was ambassador in Iraq there was limited opportunity for 'time out' before decisions. When William was balancing clarity and conviction he adopted some of the following approaches

> 'I would sometimes make a firm proposition and then see what reactions there were to this. I would talk the decision through with a few key people and see what their perspectives were. When I was given advice it was a matter of probing the analysis. Decision-making became quicker and quicker as clarity about facts became sharper. Key aspects were clarity about objectives, building trust, understanding the context and being clear with my colleagues about the consequences.'

For William Patey the starting point was getting as close as he could to the facts but then recognising that he only had some of the facts. You then have to make a decision on the basis of the information you have got.

William Patey's view was that he had to have confidence in his own judgement, but when exercising that judgement a key test was, 'How will I explain to the Parliamentary Foreign Affairs Select Committee if this goes wrong, why I took the decision I did?' This type of question forced him to be very clear about why he was reaching a judgement about the next action. He commented,

> *'Having that sort of question in your mind ensures that you have a clear rationale. You always have varying degrees of facts. You will never have the full range of facts available to you. But as Head of Mission there is no one else to make the decision. It is my responsibility to run my job. I rightly have no one to pass the buck to.'*

A leader of major infrastructure projects

Norman Haste has led major infrastructure projects in the UK and overseas such as the Sizewell B Nuclear Power Station, the Second Severn River Crossing and Terminal 5 at Heathrow Airport. In leading big infrastructure projects clarity is the first requirement. He aims to structure the decision-making as carefully as possible. His stages are:

- define the objectives clearly;
- consider the options available to you to deliver those objectives;
- match each of the options as closely as possible against the objectives;
- understand the totality of risks, trying to engage with what you do not know as well as what you do know;
- be mindful of the consequences of particular decisions;
- make a decision recognising that you have considered the facts that you have and do not go into a decision blindly.

For Norman, understanding the totality of the risks included: watching the political and economic factors, and analysing the potential consequences of significant political and economic conditions such as major increases in fuel costs. But he sets alongside clarity the importance of conviction. Aspects of conviction for him are:

- the quality of available experience: his belief is that intellectual horse-power is no substitute for the wisdom of experience;

- the capability of the engineering company to deliver results and the quality of the people within it;
- the confidence that your organisation can do the job well;
- a judgement about whether the engineering organisation will go forward with total commitment, as having cold feet part way through the process cannot be afforded;
- the determination and commitment within the organisation to ensure that a project once committed will be delivered.

Norman quotes the advice of a former mentor, *'If you think a project is bigger than you are you will fail.'* For Norman, conviction is crucially about not being half-hearted and having done your homework about the facts.

He talks of an international project where the prize is great, as are the risks. If the project goes wrong the reputational damage will be enormous in that part of the world. The client is setting aggressive timetables but the prize in terms of profitability is considerable. The decision comes down to the conviction issue of whether the organisation has the determination and commitment to make the project succeed and deliver a significant financial return for the business.

Norman sets out wise advice about how leaders can be prepared to take decisions based on this balance of clarity and conviction. He says that the prerequisites are:

- create an environment where individuals do not feel it is career threatening if they get a decision wrong;
- train people effectively about objectivity, risk analysis and testing options while encouraging brainstorming as a means of covering problems from a variety of difference perspectives;
- support developing leaders to enable them to make decisions effectively. Don't leave them just to their own devices. Create an atmosphere where individuals are encouraged to discuss options with others;
- have advisers on tap to encourage and coach individuals but not to tell them what to do;
- create a non-threatening environment where there is both clear accountability for decisions and practical support available;
- provide a range of sources of external advice so that fresh thinking is always available; and
- make it clear that for all big decisions, 'We are all in it together' so that an atmosphere of mutual trust is encouraged.

Norman describes decisions about a commitment to a major capital project as relatively straightforward. Once there is a commitment to build a capital project there is a clear target. In the manufacturing world it may well be a moving target as customer preferences can be very fickle. The decision to market a particular product is dependent on assumptions about the size of the market which may rapidly prove to be an inaccurate estimate. A decision in these circumstances, however thorough the analysis, is based on a conviction about what will happen to the market. Experience, an awareness of customer perspectives and a feel for the way the market is going are essential prerequisites of success where clarity of fact can only make a limited, but essential, contribution to decisions.

A hospital surgeon in Africa

Philip, a hospital surgeon working in south west Africa, has to balance clarity and conviction on a daily basis. He is faced with a multitude of individuals seeking his surgical skills and has to make difficult decisions about who he will operate upon. Often he is bringing to bear a sense of conviction about whether an individual is likely to have the will (and personal resources such as adequate nutrition and freedom from intercurrent diseases) to recover if they are subject to a complicated operation. Will there be enough health care available to ensure the individual recovers effectively from the operation?

Philip will rarely have much information about an individual's previous medical history and will never have a range of consultants whose opinions he can seek. He has to make a decision on the available information and trust his own judgement which for him is professionally fulfilling. He comments that in Western medicine the tendency to seek a second opinion may be an abdication of responsibility by the surgeon to make a decision on the basis of the facts available to them and the experience they have of similar situations. He talks of the visit by a senior Western consultant who he hoped would help him with the diagnosis of some difficult issues. The visiting consultant in most cases found it very difficult to offer definitive advice; he was missing the network of other professionals in a Western hospital with whom he would have discussed a particular situation. The visiting consultant was struck by the willingness of Philip to be decisive in a Third World country where medical needs far outstripped the supply of experienced medical consultant input.

The generic lesson in talking with Philip was the consequence of being in a situation where evidence is limited and individuals may be seeing a doctor when the illness is well advanced. When our temptation is to seek more and more information rather than make a decision, it might be helpful to have in our mind the picture of a doctor in a Third World country with a queue of patients making major decisions on the basis of quite limited information.

The chief executive of a dispersed national organisation

Bill is chief executive of an organisation with offices across the UK who talks of his action when he became concerned about the way a major project on business transformation was going. He became increasingly concerned that the project would overspend and not deliver even though the senior responsible officer and the project director were saying that the project was fine. Certain factual pieces of information and other directors' concerns, made Bill conscious that there was growing evidence of a problem.

Bill asked for reviews which produced evidence of major issues and set out clear proposals. The intellectual bit was not the problem: reviews were the obvious next step with the results confirming his concerns. The difficult part was talking with the senior responsible officer and the project director to persuade them that change was needed. Bill was convinced that radical action was necessary so he created a new programme structure and put different people in charge.

For Bill the first stage was looking carefully at some worrying facts about limited progress and the conviction that something was wrong. The second stage was rigorous scrutiny with the third stage decisive action, even when the existing leadership was consistently saying that the problem was in the process of being sorted. Bill had to have belief in his own judgement about the existence of delivery problems, the problems with the current leadership and the best way of creating a new impetus for success.

A supermarket junior manager

James talks of a need to balance clarity and conviction in a very different context. James is a junior manager in a supermarket where pilfering is a major problem. His dilemma is how do you judge whether someone has made a genuine error or is trying to cheat the system? It is relatively easy with those individuals who try to cheat the system on a regular basis. But the astute thief will be moving from store to store using a variety of means to conceal the items they are taking and do not intend to pay for.

The CCTV cameras provide data which gives clues that are often an indicator of a problem rather than providing categoric evidence. The assistants at the checkout tills are trained to observe carefully and watch for irregularities. But the thief who plans carefully may be aiming to create an aura of trust to hide their deception.

For James it is a matter of building the facts in terms of obvious evidence of theft linked with the CCTV evidence, but it is also being willing to challenge people when you are conscious that the situation does not add up and you have clear grounds of suspicion. Even if the individual does not admit an offence, once challenged they are unlikely to return to the supermarket for a period.

As a junior manager he has to keep a careful watch and ask his checkout assistants to be on their guard. He will be willing to give the customer the benefit of the doubt, but where there are repeating patterns the conviction that there is something amiss is grounds enough to ask difficult questions and bring in his supermarket manager.

The balance between clarity and conviction

The examples above deliberately come from a variety of different spheres and illustrate decisions at a range of different levels. For each of them clarity and conviction go hand in hand. Clear thinking is not only about handling facts it is also about interpreting the range of different information available to you. It is about reaching a judgement on the capabilities of individuals and whether success is likely to happen.

You can become attuned to making difficult decisions. You look for pieces of the jigsaw. You look for patterns in the information available to you. You develop an eye for making the right judgement. Sometimes you put the decision on one side and come back to it. Then something falls into place and you are comfortable with the decision you have made.

The following are key questions when weighing up the balance between clarity and conviction.

Clarity
• What are the key facts available to you?
• What are the main objectives you are trying to deliver?
• Are the options clear and do they mesh in well with the objectives?
• What are the key risks and how damaging might they be?
• How significant would success be?

Conviction
• How confident are you that the desired outcomes are right?
• What does your experience tell you about the likelihood of success?
• Is there the capability and will to implement the decision effectively?
• Do you know what your line will be if the decision goes wrong: can you justify to a reasonable independent observer the decision you took?

- Are you clear that you have a next step that is consistent with your values and where you can honestly say that, having weighed up the information available to you, you are in a position to make a sound judgement?

Balancing clarity and conviction
- To what extent is your judgement of the facts and your intuition in line?
- Are there some overwhelming facts that mean your intuition is not that relevant?
- If you gave full reign to your 'instincts' where would that take you: do you want to go there?
- What have you learnt from your previous experience of balancing clarity and conviction?
- How does your perception of a particular issue compare with the perspective of others you trust?

Next steps

Having looked at some of the dilemmas people face in balancing clarity and conviction the next two chapters look in turn at these two themes and how best to use and develop our capabilities in these areas.

Chapter 2

Clarity

A key starting point for any decision-making is clarity. Achieving clarity embraces several steps including: objectivity about the issue, defining the problem well, being clear on the context, sound analysis, focused objectives, defined options and sound risk analysis. It also involves handling complexity, living with compromises and working through consequences. Clarity is about trying to find simplicity in the face of complexity and knowing when to say enough information is enough.

Figure 2.1 sets out a sequence of steps to help ensure clarity in decision-making. This sequence is built around three, key defining areas of clarity: the issue, the analysis and the way ahead. It is rarely a straightforward progression through these elements but time spent clarifying the issue and then working through the analysis is rarely wasted. It is a matter of maintaining momentum, keeping up the resolve to get to clarity about the way ahead, and knowing when to crystallise options and when to compromise.

CLARITY
The Essential Steps

THE ISSUE

Be Objective about the Issues
↓
Define the Problem
↓
Be Clear on the Context
↓

THE ANALYSIS

Ensure Sound Analysis
↓
Live with Complexity
↓
Ensure Sound Structure
↓
Do Sound Risk Analysis
↓

THE WAY
FORWARD

Have Focused Objectives
↓
Define Clear Options
↓
Know When to Compromise
↓
Triangulate Your Views With Others
↓
Work Through Consequences
↓
Strive for Simplicity
↓
Be Aware of the Pitfalls

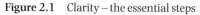

Figure 2.1   Clarity – the essential steps

The issue

This covers being objective about the issues, defining the problem and being clear on the context.

Be objective about the issues

This section draws out the views of leaders from different spheres about bringing objectivity to decision-making. They wrestle with the limits of objectivity.

Their starting point is always about bringing as much objectivity as possible. Of course we are objective, we say to ourselves, but are we? Jane Willis, a director in a UK regulatory body reflects,

> 'It is important to take out prejudice, bias and baggage when it comes to making decisions. For most decisions what is important is getting clarity about the facts, being clear what you think is right, and understanding the politics and what is the context. The more senior you go the more you have to take account of the political environment. Tuning in to the reality of the wider political environment is so crucial at senior levels.'

Chris Banks is founder of the food and drink company, Big Thoughts. He sees a big difference in how you apply objectivity between decisions when there are a number of discrete options; decisions where there are great uncertainties; and decisions involving people. He sees merit in methodologies that bring economic factors firmly into the consideration of different options, but also reflects on the limitation of quantification. He says,

> 'When choices have to be made, for example in setting strategic priorities for investment, there are a set of numerical indicators which help bring clarity to the decision-making process. But sometimes there are so many uncertainties that any form of quantification becomes difficult and potentially meaningless. At this point over-elaboration of quantified indicators can give a semblance of objectivity to a decision where there is in fact only a limited amount of clarity.'

Chris sees the most difficult decisions as those where there are consequences for people, where trying to be as objective as possible is important,

'It is relatively straightforward to say I know what is best for the business, but much more difficult when you have to consider the people implications. But objectivity is equally important when it comes to decisions about people for as soon as you make decisions on the basis of making people happy you are into all sorts of difficulties.'

Peter Drucker in 'The Effective Decision' (*Harvard Business Review*, 1967, January–February edition) took the view that,

'Effective executives do not make a great many decisions. They concentrate on what is important. They try to make the few important decisions on the highest level of conceptual understanding. They try to find the constant in a situation, to think through what is strategic and generic rather than to "solve problems". They are, therefore, not overly impressed by speed in decision-making; rather they consider virtuosity and manipulating a great many variables a symptom of sloppy thinking. They want to know what the decision is all about and what the underlying realities are which it has to satisfy. They want impact rather than technique and they want to be sound rather than clever.'

For Drucker the effective decision maker knows when a decision has to be based on principle and when it should be made pragmatically on the merits of the case. He is also aware that the trickiest decisions are between the right and the wrong compromise and that the action commitment should be as close as possible to the capacity of the people that will have to carry it out.

Objectivity is not a simple, easy answer. It involves defining the right level of detail relevant for this decision and sticking at that level, clarity about the wider context of the financial, political or media environment, and a clear understanding of the framework of both timescales and accountabilities.

Define the problem

Defining the problem is a crucial next step. It might be a generic problem or one that is exceptional and new. It could be addressing a problem which has occurred for the first time and might be in danger of recurring on a regular basis.

John Suffolk who is the UK Government's chief information officer with wide experience of leadership in the public and private sector is clear that,

'In making difficult decisions the key issue is to be absolutely clear what the problem is. So often there is a lack of clarity about the nature of the problem and the type of decision that needs to be made. The key thing is to bring the head and the heart together. The strand of what is possible is an important one in enabling facts to be weighed up in a meaningful way.'

John Gieve, a deputy governor at the Bank of England, echoes the importance of looking carefully at the nature of the problem. He says,

'Some are intellectual problems, others are motivational problems. The most complex are often decisions on structures which will have consequences long after you have forgotten them by embedding new incentives in an organisation by affecting money, organisation, and the performance matrix. These are important because you can't always predict the consequences on the performance of the organisation and on individuals.'

The lesson from so many situations is that time invested in bringing clarity about the nature of the problem is essential groundwork for ensuring the right issues are being tackled. It can be so easy to accept a problem at face value and not get behind it and dissect it.

Where significant groundwork has gone into analysing the problem decisions can be implemented the more quickly because the problem has been anticipated in advance.

Be clear on the context

No decision can be made in isolation. Every decision has knock-on consequences. To ignore or block out the wider environment can bring a clarity in addressing a problem. But without a sensitivity to the context the history, the personalities, and the political and economic environment there can be a foolhardiness in decision-making.

Justin McCracken, who has held various senior positions in regulatory bodies, uses as an example a plant in North West England where waste chemicals were burnt as a fuel in the making of cement. The experts were convinced it was acceptable but they did not explain it effectively and had not engaged with local politicians and local people. They quickly had the press against them and everyone else was lined up against them: the result was massive political controversy. The firm had created a context where everyone was against the decision to increase the use of the toxic chemicals. Because the firm had not taken account of the context or built bridges with the community there were huge protests and they lost both the emotional and the intellectual argument.

The self-discipline of an individual or a team in standing back and looking at the wider context is an important step before any decision of significance is taken so that issue, problem and context are looked at in a considered way together.

The analysis

The analysis phase is about sound analysis, living with complexity, ensuring a sound structure and giving priority to effective risk analysis.

Ensure sound analysis

Sound analysis must be about addressing the facts, with facts coming in all shapes and sizes. The importance of sound analysis is central for Linda Freestone who was a deputy District Judge and is currently an Immigration Judge. How does she do sound analysis?

> 'As a deputy District Judge in a Magistrate's Court I have to make rapid decisions. I arrive in court early, study the list of cases and do some research on the ones that look difficult. It is then my job to listen very carefully to the advocates and not let the variation in the quality of the way the advocates present influence the way I assess the arguments. Some of the most difficult decisions I make are about custodial sentences when I am having to weigh up the facts very carefully. What helps me most is to sit at my laptop and write down the key factors. As I do this I become clearer in my mind as to the next steps. Writing down the key factors helps me strip away some of the peripheral issues. It enables me to be clear what I have to decide and in which direction the key factors point.'

For Linda part of weighing up the facts is being intensively engaged with the written arguments and the oral presentations. But sound analysis is also Linda giving herself space to stand back. She comments,

> 'I think best when I have a moment of quiet. Therefore sometimes I will ask the Court to rise for a few moments and I will go into a quiet room. It is in those moments of reflection that I crystallise my conclusions.'

Sound analysis is not always an ordered process. It can be like piecing together information in the form of a jigsaw puzzle. Suddenly you see a connection and two pieces of information sit together. Gradually the picture comes into focus with a range of elements from different sources. Progress comes as one element is added to another and in rather a disordered way the jigsaw becomes complete.

Sound analysis depends both on seeing a wider context and also not allowing leakage to take place so that the emotions about one set of decisions influence another decision. Archie Hughes who has held senior positions in the aeronautics industry in both the public and private sector is clear that,

> 'When you have to take hard decisions you have to take out the personal dimension. It is important to compartmentalise things into boxes, then personal judgement becomes less skewed.'

While sound analysis is an essential precursor of good decisions, it can sometimes lead to 'analysis paralysis'. On other occasions a hesitancy about sound analysis can lead to haphazardness. Martin Oakley, a senior lawyer at Reuters, talks of individuals sometimes making life difficult for themselves through a sense of disregard of important information. He comments that sometimes people seem to avoid taking difficult decisions by just being careless about them. A 'fear' of analysis can lead to the avoidance of key facts and resulting random decisions. This distancing from analysis could result from a hesitancy about where analysis might lead or even a fear of unforeseen outcomes. But the facts in a sound analysis are not just about figures. It is about building an accurate picture through acute observation.

Gill Lucas is a headhunter greatly trusted by those seeking new senior executives. She always gives a clear perspective about a job and whether it might be suitable for an individual. There is never any putting on a particular gloss or trying to influence people in an unreasonable way. She always states the facts clearly and thoughtfully. The consequence is she builds relationships of trust very quickly. When she meets an individual she consciously does not make a quick judgement but lets the discussion flow. She thinks carefully about what she hears and observes clearly how somebody describes their situation and how they reflect on individual people and circumstances. She is using all her powers of observation. It is about analysing all the data she receives on paper, from other individuals and from the person she is talking to and then assessing as clearly as she can whether that individual has the right capabilities and character to fit a particular job.

When dealing with complex situations, the purist view of focusing solely on the importance of analysis can come unstuck, because analysis can only take you so far. Nicky Munroe, a former director general within the Scottish Executive, comments that,

'The easier decisions are when the answer is a straight yes or no. It is much more difficult where there is lack of clarity and where the consequences are not entirely clear. It is in these complex situations where it is most difficult to reach a judgement. Where the situation is complex the answer is a combination of as much clarity as you can, then the courage to take forward what you believe is right even though you enter a period of criticism.'

Complexity is not a reason to avoid making a decision. It may be a reason for more information, or involving a range of people in a decision, or piloting a particular answer but it is not a reason for avoidance. Being honest about the degree of complexity, the limitations of knowledge and the degree of uncertainty in the chosen course are prerequisites to making decisions in complex situations. Decisions are becoming ever more complex in the commercial environment. This has been fuelled by many things including: commercial organisations themselves becoming ever more complicated, the effect of globalisation bringing another dimension of complication in terms of legislative, financial and cultural differences, the speed of availability of information, the increased interconnectedness of different decisions, and the intensity of competition. The experience in many sectors is the same. Complexity is foisted upon us by the modern world but we then make our processes ever more complicated partially because we have the IT capacity to do so, partially as a means of staying ahead, but sometimes just as a means of demonstrating we are clever.

The plea to enable decision-making to take account of an ever more complex world is admirable, often necessary, but is sometimes undermining and destructive of good decisions. John, a senior executive in a fast moving industry, tries to keep his focus on identifying patterns in complexity. His belief is that with any set of complex considerations there ought to be some guiding principles which can turn complexity into a discernible pattern. His motto in any complex situation is, can we crystal this down to the three key problems:

- the principles against which we should make a judgement;
- clarity about what is a successful outcome;
- building a simple clear story about next steps.

His message is about complexity being an opportunity to find a line of sight through a wealth of data.

For us, living with complexity is a given whether we like it or not. Part of the answer is accepting that complexity is a fact of life and will not go away! But we can look for patterns, apply principles and accept that we will have to try to simplify our next steps. Ensuring sound structures when decisions are difficult or complicated is an essential part of the process, but one which brings with it its own inherent dangers. Clear structures allow for factors to be weighed up carefully, stakeholders to be involved, analysis to be considered and options to be tested out.

John Gieve talks of structures as an important way of enabling a leader to clear their own mind and build an agreed pathway ahead. He comments,

> *'You institutionalise things. You set up structures and ensure you take the necessary time to listen to other people. You create space with your team to work through the issues.'*

Key tests in assessing any structure which is used in making difficult decisions are:

- are the right range of people participating?
- is it clear where the ultimate authority for the decision lies?
- does the process provide for the appropriate mix of data to be considered?
- is an independent view adequately built in to the process?
- is the timetable compatible with both the external constraints and the capacity of the individuals involved? is there a feedback loop so the processes can be continually improved?
- is it clear what success looks like in terms of whether the structure has worked adequately?

Do sound risk analysis

One way of addressing complexity is through sound risk analysis, drawing on both the perspective of key players and external individuals looking at the issues from an independent perspective. Archie Hughes has had to take a range of calculated risks in his leadership roles within the aeronautical industry. He says,

> *'Every choice is a risk. Decision-making needs to be seen in the context of risk management. You need to recognise when you are taking subconscious decisions about the scope of risks you are prepared to make. Some people are very calculating about risk. There is the personal exposure element of risk linked to an individual's capacity to be clear in their thinking and courageous in their decisions.'*

Sound risk taking involves the effective use of external experts. The good expert will command credibility and respect from others both inside and outside the organisation. They can bring a wealth of experience from which they can draw inferences and pose key questions. The expert can help identify patterns but too much deference to experts under the banner of reducing risk can sap independence of thought and creativity in a way which can be counterproductive. Beware the expert who knows the answer to every question. Welcome the expert who can enable you to ask the right questions. Watch whether too much of a focus on experts can undermine the commitment of team members to solve problems if there has been limited opportunity for team members to express their perspective in reaching key decisions.

Mairi Eastwood, the managing partner at Praesta Partners, focuses on living with uncertainties when making decisions at senior levels in legal firms. In a recent article in *Legal Week* she writes about lawyers with good analytic skills struggling to handle risk well. She comments,

> 'Understandably, given that law is all about precision, there has always been greater emphasis on minimising risk. So it is a tough transition to move out of that comfort zone into a role that requires both creating a vision for staff and partners to follow and taking commercial decisions where uncertainty is a fact of life.'

One of the biggest changes a leader makes as they move up tiers in leadership is handling risk well. The amount of information they know becomes less and less, while the significance of the decisions increase. So having sound risk analysis in place becomes an important source of reassurance.

The way forward

Key elements in clarity about the way forward include having:

- focused objectives,
- defining clear options,
- knowing when to compromise,
- triangulating your views with others,
- working through consequences,
- striving for simplicity and being aware of pitfalls.

Have focused objectives

Clarity in decision-making becomes easier if there are clear overall objectives. When an individual or organisation has 20 objectives the heart sinks.

Can that organisation or individual be clear what their purposes are? Can they explain them in such a way that a customer, investor or stakeholder can both comprehend what the organisation is aiming to do, and articulate it clearly and simply in their own mind?

The leader's role is often to articulate a set of clear overall objectives, to help others develop clear objectives or to provide a wider perspective or a line of sight through to the long-term strategy. The leader's role can then be to ensure that the clarity of vision is not lost in a welter of detail.

John Gieve talks of his role in bringing steadiness of purpose in reaching agreed objectives as Permanent Secretary at the Home Office when it was setting up the National Offender Management Service bringing together the work of the Probation Service and the Prison Service. He comments,

> 'The debate was whether we should pursue this radically different approach or not. I was a strong supporter and did think it was the right thing to do. Probation and prisons needed to work more closely together. My role was as a queller of doubting voices: in a sense I provided steadiness of purpose. I needed to provide some steady support as people developed the framework as it was the details that could derail.'

In my first career in the civil service I worked closely with Kenneth Baker and David Blunkett. Both brought very clear objectives to their leadership as Secretary of State for Education. Kenneth Baker's legacy was about greater delegation to schools and colleges. David Blunkett's was about a strong focus on school standards. Both had very clear explicit objectives which helped to ensure their success.

Define clear options

Decision-making can sometimes get stuck in a triangle between ever more complicated analysis of the information, increasingly sophisticated working through risk, and debate about whether objectives are sustainable. Breaking the stalemate often comes through identifying options and seeing the extent to which they meet the different objectives. The specification of options can help bring clarity about the way forward with some options falling by the wayside because they do not stack up whilst others gradually gain in plausibility. If a decision has to be made by a specific deadline the mind is inevitably focused on the options. Sometimes it is an external deadline which creates this focus. On other occasions we can create an artificial deadline which can have the same effect of giving a clearer reality to different options. The way out of a difficult issue may well be through examining a series of options. But sometimes the focus on different options can ignore the option of the 'doing nothing' option. Sometimes no action is the right action while await-ing new information or insights. A breathing space can be highly desirable before any major decision. But in the words of John Suffolk, with his exten-sive experience of leadership in the public and private sectors,

> *'Often it is better to take a decision than not take one. Often the key thing is to get individuals to a position where they are willing to make a decision.'*

Uncertainty can be damaging, undermining of confidence and detrimen-tal to the ability to make further decisions. If a decision is not taken the drift of events can lead to accepting the inevitable, which nobody is seeking.

Know when to compromise

A strong focus on clarity implies that there is a right answer to every ques-tion, but sometimes there is no right answer. We sometimes regard 'com-promise' as a dirty word, but it is an inevitable part of many decision-mak-ing processes. There are some occasions when compromise is out of the question, for example when fixed points are part of the decision-making process. It could be absolute requirements on safety, standards of honesty and financial proprietary or values in the way individuals are treated.

Justin McCracken, drawing from his experience as a senior leader in both the chemical industry and in regulatory bodies, talks of clarity leading to compromise.

> *'It is crucial to be clear about the strategic aims and objectives and what we are trying to do. Decisions involve compromise so the key thing is where do you make compromises. Having strategic aims and objectives enables you to judge whether a compromise is right. Knowing what the priorities are helps you to make trade- offs.'*

At a fairly simple level a compromise might be about the choice to buy a new 'off-the-shelf' information system because to design a new system from scratch would be too costly. Sometimes the trade-offs can be easily costed but at other times it is much less certain. Is pragmatism a dirty com-promise or is it acknowledging the reality of a situation? However strong the plea for clarity, most decisions involve an element of compromise based on pragmatism. Making a decision work often involves a degree of compro-mise. When you are mediating between powerful groups it is no good just being right and sitting on your dignity. Sometimes when you make difficult decisions you have to trim them.

Triangulate your views with others.

An important check on clarity comes from triangulating your views with others. You may be clear about next steps but what is the perspective of those you trust? Those whose judgement you trust may be critics as well as allies.

However, getting an accurate perspective from a range of viewpoints can be invaluable in moving towards soundly based next steps. Paul Connew is a financial director with extensive experience of the public and private sectors. He comments,

> *'In order to establish clarity of thought you must not be a lone ranger. To make the correct decision you need to be in an environment in which there are a range of people bringing different skills and working in a team. The synergies of a team kick in to help make effective decisions. Teamwork is crucial at whatever level you are.'*

Valid perspectives can come from boss, peer, colleague, stakeholder or customer. Clarity on next steps can always be enhanced by seeking a diversity of views and then testing out emerging conclusions with a diversity of individuals whose views you either trust or regard as important.

Work through consequences

A good decision is not just about the consequences tomorrow or the immediately following day. For government ministers, success should not be measured just by the views of the media in tomorrow's newspaper. For commercial organisations success should not just be seen as the immediate movement in the share price. Good decisions involve looking at both the short- and long-term consequences. It is about looking thoroughly at the implications of each of the options. What might a government policy change mean for our children and our children's children? Some consequences can be uncertain and long term but attempting to evaluate the consequences can bring a different perspective to making good decisions.

In the commercial world shareholders are rarely interested in the long-term effect on the share price; so often their concern is with the value now. Increasingly businesses are trying to look at decisions with triple dimensions covering economic capital, social capital and environmental capital. The far-sighted company will not just be basing its decisions on economic return. In terms of its social capital it will be looking at how trust and reputation are built into its economic value.

Environmental considerations are becoming much more critical in business decisions with this dimension having gathered momentum in recent years. A fascinating issue over the next few years is: what are the levers that will influence commercial organisations taking environmental factors more strongly into their decision-making? It is likely to be a combination of legislative and economic factors on the one hand and reputational and value-based factors on the other. The effect of the media on decisions affecting the environment will also be an interesting test of how much identifying long-term consequences can influence effective decision-making.

A very different type of example of the consequences of decisions are those made by a prison governor. A governor whose decision turns out to be wrong is inevitably in the limelight. If a prison governor lets out an individual on temporary release who then commits a murder, the governor could be subject to disciplinary action. The concern of the prison governor when a decision is taken to allow someone out on a temporary release is, 'If this goes wrong, am I likely to be pilloried in the *Daily Mail?*'. This concern about the consequence if you get the decision wrong puts a tremendous pressure on a prison governor to get a decision right or not to take the risk in the first place. But, if the movement back to work by a prisoner is successful and they are rehabilitated, then the gain for the individual and society is enormous and well worth the risk of early release.

Looking at the consequences of a decision can be a major plus in terms of reinforcing the merits of making a particular decision, but it can be a source of inhibition if the fear of consequences leads to indecision. Looking at the positive consequences systematically against potential downsides can be an important aid to reaching a point of decision when an individual has been stuck without clarity for a while.

Strive for simplicity

A key element of clarity is searching for simplicity. Archie Hughes' perspective on striving for simplicity is,

> *'Clarity is about strength: it is important to have absolute clarity of purpose. It is about responding quickly when you need to, getting on somebody's wavelength and not being ponderous. When the leader sets a direction it is being very careful not to use the 'but' word. It is looking for the mood music. Clarity and simplicity go together. If the leader is emphasising clarity of purpose, I will respond with the same language'*

Michael Roberto in an influential article on 'Making Difficult Decisions in Turbulent Times' in the *Ivey Business Journal* (2002, January–February edition) talked of the importance of simplification. Most executives find ways to cope with uncertainty by adopting strategies to simplify complex situations so that they can make decisions quickly and effectively. Some of these strategies involve avoidance, be it of facts, situations or emotions. Michael Roberto identifies means of simplifying decisions in the following way:

1 **reasoning by analogy:** drawing from past experiences when faced with a complex problem;
2 **imitation:** emulating the strategies and practices of other highly successful organisations;
3 **applying rules of thumb:** using a simplifying measure (e.g. mortgage lenders assuming that consumers should spend no more than a particular percentage of their income on mortgage payments);
4 **reformulation:** reframing one complex problem as a sequence of smaller problems enabling small wins to be achieved in order to build up momentum towards achieving the objective of solving the overall problem.

These four approaches are based on attempts to simplify the issues in a way which is manageable for the individual trying to take a difficult decision. It might be worth developing a simplifying approach when you are deciding how to handle a mass of analysis. However, too much of a focus on simplicity does have its dangers. Roger Martin in his recent article entitled 'How successful leaders think' talks of a desire for simplicity sometimes meaning that interesting and novel solutions are ignored. His perspective is that the integrative decision maker will welcome and work with complexity to try to find new solutions and move on from predictable and unattractive solutions. A key practical issue for us in decision-making is how we balance the search for simplicity with the recognition of complexity. Questions might be:

- How far down can I simplify the issues?
- Am I taking enough account of the complexity involved?
- Can I take advantage of the complexity to come up with new and innovative approaches?

Be aware of pitfalls

There can never be absolute clarity in making difficult decisions but sometimes we compound the difficulties. Some pitfalls can be avoided by following certain strategies.

Make it impersonal

Saying that you disagree with an argument can lead more quickly to an
agreed conclusion than saying you disagree with an individual.

Mary tells the story of a discussion in the senior team about the payment
of bonuses. James had given all his direct reports a recommended bonus
whereas Hazel had been much tougher in her assessment. Mary said that
she disagreed with James and agreed with Hazel. Her reflection was that,
if she had talked of agreeing with one particular approach with no reference to who had advocated that approach, it could have led more quickly
to an effective outcome. An even better approach might have been to talk
neutrally about the threshold at which the bonus level was set.

The importance of seeing the bigger picture

The desire for clarity in reaching a decision can drive the decision maker
into ever more detailed analysis and take them further and further away
from the original strategic objective. Where the burrowing down becomes
extreme it can mean the individual ending up in a hole of their own making
where their wider perspective has completely disappeared.

Continually coming back to the bigger picture is a prerequisite of good
decision-making.

Watch the instant decision

Sometimes a decision may seem easy and straightforward. The instant
answer 'No' is given when perhaps there might have been an opportunity
briefly to stand back and reflect. Life is full of instant decisions, for example
when we are driving a car. The trick is discrimination between instant decisions done almost on autopilot, and the instant decision that might benefit
from a little bit of reflection. We often take a lot of decisions automatically
because we have forgotten how to look at a problem from different angles.

Watch bureaucracy

Consistency in the way in which individual people are treated is important
in any organisation. But the result can sometimes be a mass of systems and
processes. Arrangements that provide fairness and protection are always

legitimate but sometimes counterproductive. The prison governor Eoin McLennan-Murray tells the delightful story of how he had been prepared to take a risk in enabling a prisoner to get their first job cleaning telephone boxes on a temporary release. The individual then got promoted to supervisor and eventually set up their own car hire business after leaving prison. The joy of the original decision to give temporary release was seeing the individual make a success of a new life.

Don't let emotions get in the way

Emotions such as the desire for approval or fear of failure can get in the way of effective decision-making. The consequence of risks in decision-making is that they create anxieties, with those anxieties becoming a potential source of distortion. Irving Janis and Leon Mann in their book, *Decision Making* (1979, Detroit: Free Press) talk of patterns of emotional reaction to decisions including defensive avoidance (delaying decisions unduly), overreaction (making decisions impulsively in order to escape the anxious state) and hyper-vigilance (obsessively collecting more and more information instead of making a decision).

Being conscious of emotional reactions to decision-making is the starting point to addressing such reactions and minimising the distortion which they create. This is addressed further in Chapter 3.

Beware overreacting to excessive information

Amitai Etzioni in his article entitled 'Humble Decision-making' (*Harvard Business Review*, 1989, July–August edition) suggests that having to cope with too much information and too little time creates the dangers of either incrementalism or full-steam ahead. He perceives incrementalism as the science of muddling through which advocates moving not so much towards a goal as away from trouble, trying this or that small manoeuvre without any ground plan or sense of ultimate purpose. Invariably the effect is a direction close to the prevailing one without radical options being considered. Etzioni sees the opposite danger as steaming full ahead: remaking the world rather than seeking to understand it, with executives advised not to sit back and await sufficient information but to pick the course favoured by their experience and then pump in enough resources to prove the decision right. Etzioni advocates an approach which accepts proceeding with partial information. He calls it mixed scanning (or humble) decision-making involving two sets of judgements, namely broad choices about an organisation's goals and policies and small experimental decisions based on in-depth examination of particular facts and choices. He describes the best analogy as the approach taken by doctors who use a mixed scanning approach of considering the general health of a patient and then focusing in through different investigative approaches on a particular complaint.

The relevance of Etzioni's approach is to be cautious of how we respond to excessive information. Standing back and trying to identify key themes has to be the right approach.

Next steps

The search for clarity is at the centre of all decision-making. But there are many different aspects, which mean it is never as simple as searching after the simple truth. So much depends on the context, the nature of the problem, the degree of complexity, the need for compromise, the nature of the consequences. Key themes in applying clarity are about the search for simplicity, an awareness of the pitfalls and honest and rigorous objectivity untainted by emotional reactions. It might be worth reflecting on:

- What part does clarity play in the way you make decisions?
- What is the best way for you of ensuring objectivity in the way you take decisions?
- In what area do you need to make progress in building clarity further into the way you make decisions?
- What will success look like in six months in terms of how you ensure seeking clarity is fully built into your approach to decision-making.

Chapter 3

Conviction

Making difficult decisions is not just about the straightforward weighing up of facts. However good the information and analysis may seem there is something else going on in our minds when a decision needs to be taken. We bring to any decision a starting perspective, an intuition or a gut feeling. Sometimes this provides insights and enables us to interpret facts in a constructive way. Sometimes it means we bring the baggage of previous experience and an emotional perspective that is blinkered.

A key issue is how we use that sense of conviction in a constructive way. How do we recognise when it is a plus and when it is in danger of sending us down a blind alley? Conviction can be criticised as non-objective, prejudice or a means of escape from reality. Conviction can fall into the trap of being any of these three things. Testing whether conviction is helpful or dangerous is crucial or else we fall into a spiral of self-deception. Conviction is an asset when based on good understanding. It needs to be accompanied by honesty and the ability to analyse your own thinking. If conviction becomes dogma it can blind us to reality. Conviction needs to be continually assessed and tested.

Conviction comes from a number of different elements such as intuitive judgement, the relevance of values, the significance of past experience, trained judgement, and emotional awareness (Figure 3.1).

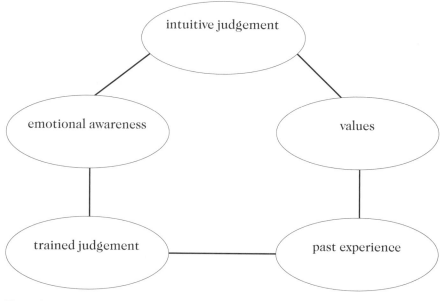

Figure 3.1 Conviction: the key elements.

This chapter goes through each of these strands of conviction and then looks at approaches to testing the significance of our convictions through standing back, keeping calm, the importance of conversations with colleagues, mentoring and coaching, and the awareness of key pitfalls. (Illustrated in Figure 3.2 below.)

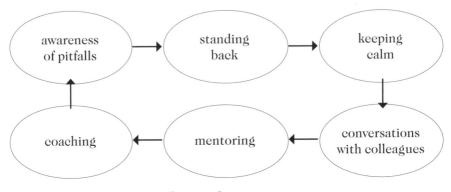

Figure 3.2 Convictions: testing their significance

The key elements

Intuitive judgement

Alden Hayashi in his article, 'When to Trust Your Gut' (*Harvard Business Review*, February 2001) suggested that emotions and feelings might not only be important in the ability to make good decisions but might actually be essential. Managers will often rely on their intuitions to solve complex problems when logical methods have not led them to a clear conclusion. The author suggests that gut calls are better suited to some functions (corporate strategy and planning, marketing, public relations, human resources and research and development) than others (production and operations management and finance). The author argues that:

- your mind is continuously processing information that you are not consciously aware of which can explain the sensation experienced when you learn something that you already knew. The 'of course' moment;
- your brain is intricately linked to other parts of the body through the nervous system which can explain why intuitive feelings are frequently

accompanied by physical reactions: a good idea is often associated with feeling physically good.

Henry Mintzberg, Professor of Management at Magill University, talks of the sense of revelation at the obvious occurring when the conscious mind finally learns something that the subconscious mind had already known. Mintzberg and others have distinguished the two kinds of thought by talking of 'left brain' for the conscious, rational and logical, and 'right brain' for the subconscious, intuitive and emotional. While these two terms are an oversimplification of the functions of the human brain, they do provide a useful reminder of how these two thought patterns sit alongside each other and how important it is to apply both perspectives in viewing an issue.

Leigh Lewis has had a sequence of leadership roles involving making difficult decisions. He was chief executive of Jobcentre Plus and is now Permanent Secretary at the UK Government Department for Work and Pensions. His reflection is,

> 'Intuition and gut feeling are important. You can sometimes reach a conclusion intellectually but intuitively feel it is wrong. As you balance analysis and intuition you sometimes need to stop and listen to the voices around you and talk to people. Sometimes some extra time can give you more perspective. Often something then happens to clarify the situation, with the result that analysis and intuition are in line.'

Stephen Timms has had extensive experience as a minister in the UK Government working in a range of different government departments. Some of the subject matter he knew well and other areas less well. His reflection is

> 'There is an interesting strand about what role intuition plays if you know varying degrees about the subject. If you are steeped in it, you have lots of experience embedded within you and therefore conviction can be based on your long-term understanding. If you are new to a topic, any sense of intuition comes from a wider perspective about how different people are likely to react.'

Government ministers moving from subject to subject have no alternative but to rely on facts prepared by others, their own judgement about who they trust and the value of parallel experience from other subject areas.

John Gieve had a full career within the Treasury and then as Permanent Secretary at the Home Office before becoming a Deputy Governor of the Bank of England. He talks of,

'the importance of analysis while still acknowledging the importance
of gut feeling. It is then a matter of trying to build in enough checks:
recognising that decision-making is not purely a rational process is im-
portant.'

The overwhelming experience of senior leaders is that intuition should
not be ignored. It is an essential element in the decision-making process. It
often provides a shortcut to a point where key factors can be exposed and
analysed in depth. Used well, intuition is a means to an end and not an end
in itself. Then, by testing out any hypothesis coolly and rationally, it is possible to assess whether the intuitive judgement is soundly based.

Anna Ford, the former TV broadcaster, talks of the judgements she had
to make at speed about whether the person she was interviewing was telling the truth. It was a matter of thinking quickly, weighing up the information she had got and reaching a judgement about whether she thought
the interviewee was hiding something. This initial judgement, plus the research she had done, would steer her questions.

The relevance of values and behaviours

A set of values in any organisation provides a framework against which
difficult decisions can be made. The following illustration shows how a set
of behaviours within an organisation helped provide a valuable framework
when difficult decisions had to be made. After an extensive consultation
period the following behaviours were introduced in 2002 into what was
then the UK Department of Education and Skills.

- We are determined to make a difference.
- We listen and value diversity.
- We are honest and open.
- We innovate and challenge.
- We learn and improve.

As a board we emphasised that the behaviours covered both hard and soft
skills. We recognised that the behaviours often needed to be linked together
where an individual was deciding on a particular course of action. Nothing could be 'harder' than 'we are determined to make a difference'. On
the other hand 'we listen and value diversity' required all the 'soft' skills of
empathy, self-awareness, team building and effective feedback to be fully
embedded. These behaviours were central when difficult decisions had to
be taken.

When it came to taking difficult decisions about reducing staff numbers at the department, David Normington, the then Permanent Secretary, said that what kept him going was the support of the leadership team which worked it through together. Also important was the recognition that the leadership either took charge and made changes or the department would be told what was going to happen. In taking difficult decisions about staff reductions, the Board was as open as it could be with the staff. David Normington got a lot of feedback from people who may not have liked what was happening but said, 'You have done it in a way that is true to the behaviours'.

The fact that the behaviours followed extensive consultation, were lived by the Board members and were used as a touchstone for assessing next steps, is a demonstration of the importance of a behaviour or value base in implementing decisions. When decisions are taken that are clearly consistent with the behaviours, acceptance of those decisions is far more likely than would otherwise be the case.

Jane Willis, a director in a national regulatory body, talks of the importance of addressing values when making decisions. She reflected

> *'The lack of information makes decisions the hardest. You must be clear what type of hypothesis you are testing. It is an easy decision when you have a set of answers readily available. Difficult decisions are where there is a clash of values or a clash of potentially equally good options.'*

Julie Taylor who has had wide experience as a director in UK government departments talks of the importance of principles in addressing difficult decisions. She reflects that sometimes you disagree with a proposed approach based on analysis and facts, but there can be a more fundamental difference about priorities. In these situations of difference about priorities you need a set of principles in addressing difficult decisions. You have to have a principles or values framework within which to assess your analysis of the facts and decide on your response.

A conflict of values can easily apply in major investment decisions. For example how much should environmental considerations be taken into account in the investment choices about new vehicle design? Is it purely a matter of quantifying every last detail or is there a value factor which cannot be fully quantified about the importance of reducing carbon emissions? Maybe a figure can be put on most variables. Some values may be quantifiable whereas others are an act of faith such as the value attached to environmental considerations or the way particular individuals are treated.

Archie Hughes in reflecting on decisions he has taken about staff reductions and the closure of factories is clear that a moral framework is important. He sees conviction as being about honesty, compassion and empathy. It is not putting off tough decisions: it is doing them in a way where your reasons are explicit and the processes are fair. You need to have lines you don't cross and be seen not to cross those lines.

As a prison governor Eoin McLennan-Murray sees the values you reinforce in a prison as crucial. In his perspective,

> 'Within the prison the culture is important in terms of the relationship between prisoners and staff. The way people are spoken to and valued is crucial. As one prisoner said, "The more trust you are given, the harder it is to abuse it.'

But the issues are not just with prisoners. Eoin reflects that he spends more time on decisions about staff than on prisoners, with key issues arising if staff are bringing in drugs or mobile phones. His concern is, if there is a suspicion that this is being done, do I continue to let them work in the jail? It is how this type of issue is responded to that establishes the relative importance attached to values within an organisation like a prison. Where there is suspicion involving the use of drugs, Eoin has to ask himself: is the individual out of the door straightaway or is there is a subtle warning system directed at changing behaviour?

The relevance of values covers both organisational values and personal values. Organisational values can provide an invaluable framework for difficult decisions and the means of both explaining and accepting them. Honesty by an individual in assessing whether their personal values are consistent with the organisational values is important. If they are at odds decision-making is never going to be comfortable for that individual. A valuable exercise can be to tease out what values will be important in any difficult decision-making process. It can help provide a framework which relegates some of the emotional reactions to second place where the organisational values provide a sound base for decision-making.

Some individuals talk of the importance of conscience in decision-making. They see this inner barometer as an important guide in making decisions. Reference to a conscience may seem old fashioned. But maybe an individual's conscience is the summation of the values that are most important to them both from their personal and cultural history and from their own beliefs and behaviours. Allowing your conscience to speak to you can be an important check on hasty decisions.

For others, religious values are important in making difficult decisions. Young Christians often wear armbands with the letters WWJD on them.

For them 'What Would Jesus Do' is a valid question to ask when they have to make decisions. When asked why they do this they will say that this question puts the decision into perspective and makes them reflect on whether there are any principles in the way Jesus lived that are relevant to their own decisions today. Some criticise this mantra of WWJD as simplistic. For others it provides a practical and profound question that has stood the test of 2000 years: at the very least it is a prompt to careful thought.

A significant number of individuals will bring their religious understanding to bear when making difficult decisions and use approaches of quiet reflection, meditation and prayer as an aid to decision-making. This may lead to blinkering if a rigid perspective is brought, but equally bringing the wealth of understanding from different faith traditions can bring objectivity, detachment and the wisdom of long experience. It can allow values based on an understanding of human nature, forgiveness, redemption and resurrection to play a part in decision-making.

Spiritual awareness is increasingly seen as important alongside intellectual and emotional awareness. It can help give a rounded understanding as important decisions are taken, bringing to the fore the implications for the way individuals are respected and the long-term well being of individuals and communities.

The biggest danger is the playing of the 'God card' irresponsibly by religious leaders of any faith. Such attempts to impose 'God's will' in decision-making normally results from an unwillingness to engage with others. Such arrogance is normally counterproductive and gives spirituality a bad name. Outstanding religious leaders such as Basil Hume, Jonathan Sachs and Rowan Williams have influenced decisions by engaging with ideas and concerns and by bringing a perspective that is both fresh and rooted in religious and cultural history.

The significance of past experience

Past experience is both a good guide and a false teacher. Archie Hughes from the aeronautical world talks of when to draw on past experience and when to neutralise for bias. He advocates bringing tangible examples from prior experience and using analogy to help address new issues, but then being very clear in your own mind that you are not bound by what happened on previous occasions.

Justin McCracken talks of the relevance of his earlier work in the chemicals world in his current role now as a senior regulator. For him it is both drawing on his previous experience and then testing it in conversation with others. He comments,

> '*My background at ICI taught me that it was often much more impor-
> tant to take a decision than necessarily to get it absolutely right. It is
> important to be able to understand the opportunity cost of spending too
> long on some issues and not reaching others. Conviction is important.
> I have felt concerned about decisions which have gone against what my
> gut has said. A year on I have often been able to articulate why I felt
> strongly about something. The best way of testing conviction is one-
> to-one discussions with other managers. It is crucial that these discus-
> sions are in an environment where the other managers can be open
> (i.e. it is consequence free for them). I believe you can develop the best
> perspectives on decisions in conversation. I always learn from people of
> different backgrounds: what is crucial is the quality of conversation in
> working through things with them so that the perspective that comes
> from experience is tested.*'

Past experience provides invaluable data and can be a good guide. But continually testing past experience in a rapidly changing world is ignored at our peril.

The accumulation of past experience is a necessary but not sufficient element in decision-making. Past experience can be just about repeated experience which enables us to make some decisions without much thought. But where past experience leads to wisdom is where we draw associations from past experience into assessing what is possible in the present. It is when the content, context, timing and implications from previous experience come together that past experience can enable us to make a wise choice in a new situation.

Trained judgement

Sometimes the facts are not that clear or you are dealing with a decision involving human factors that cannot be quantified. Eoin McLennan-Murray, as a prison governor, talks of the difficult decisions needed with borderline cases for home detention curfew and temporary release. He comments,

> '*If I am deciding whether to let somebody go out on temporary release I
> go and see the prisoner and talk about their life and values. Then I make
> a judgement about whether to agree to home detention curfew or tem-
> porary release. The type of questions I ask myself are: Do I think they
> are being straight with me? Do they have the determination to make it
> work? Are they trustworthy? There is in one sense a methodology but
> it is a judgement too. When people make a commitment to you there
> is a human bonding. It is important to create that human bonding in*

order to generate a commitment from a prisoner to honour what they have said to you. In one sense my decisions are process driven, but my own judgement is very important.'

For Eion trained judgement is an essential part of the life of a prison governor. He has to weigh up all the risks but cannot quantify them. The pressures on prison governors push them to be cautious in decision-making because of the repercussions if a decision proves to be wrong. The balance is between the danger of a damaging tabloid headline and the opportunity to rehabilitate an offender more effectively outside the prison than inside it.

Alice Perkins held a sequence of senior leadership roles within UK government departments, including group HR director for the UK civil service. When making difficult decisions her guiding principles were that decisions should be evidence based and truthful: she always wanted to be straightforward and to be consistent with the values that are important to her. In her trained judgement this meant:

- it was important sometimes to push back when you thought a wrong decision was being taken in order to give an effective signal to others;
- it was important to help people see that the consequences of difficult decisions were not as terrifying as they might have appeared;
- you needed to be willing to be the person who said something if a decision was going in a wrong direction.

Transformation comes when people give each other courage; when someone is solid others will be solid too. People need to know that you will back them up to the hilt.

Drawing on our trained judgement is an essential part of decision-making: as a car driver we do that all the time. But allowing that judgement to be refreshed and open to new consequences is essential.

The importance of emotional awareness

Emotional awareness has two strands: awareness of our own emotions and our awareness of the emotions of others. Psychometric assessments can bring us a wealth of understanding about how we react to different situations and how we naturally make decisions. For example within the Myers Briggs approach there is a continuum on the Thinking/Feeling spectrum. Are we led by our head or by our heart? Understanding where we come from as an individual in terms of our natural way of making decisions helps us understand how we tend to address difficult situations. It helps us understand what data we pay attention to, what we see and what we tend to ignore.

Understanding how another individual makes decisions enables us to work with them the more effectively. Understanding where an individual is on the Myers Briggs spectrum of Thinking/Feeling can help us appreciate what type of data is going to be most important to them and what sort of process they are likely to go through in making a decision.

Another valuable indicator is to know where an individual is on the Myers Briggs Extraversion/Intraversion spectrum. Do they reach decisions by talking things through or do they need to go away and reflect before reaching a conclusion? You could help an 'E' to make a decision by creating space to talk through the relevant considerations with them: for an 'I' the important prerequisite is to create space for them to reflect.

In my work as a coach an effective way of preparing for a discussion is to reflect on what an individual might be thinking and feeling. Trying to get into that position of emotional awareness about an individual helps me get on the same page as them early on in a discussion. Trying to understand why somebody reacts emotionally in the way they do can be an important starting point to working effectively with them as they make decisions.

Testing the significance of convictions

The first step has been identifying the key elements of conviction covering intuitive judgement, values, past experience, trained judgement and emotional awareness. We now move into testing the significance of convictions looking at the importance of standing back, keeping calm, conversations with colleagues, mentoring, coaching and the awareness of pitfalls.

The importance of standing back

Sometimes we have to take instant decisions but it is important to create opportunities to stand back whenever possible. David Normington, the Permanent Secretary at the Home Office, talks of the importance of creating time. He comments,

> 'You take a brief look and reflect on it. It will become clearer overnight: I am happy to say I will make a decision by 9am the following day. If you get more and more tense, that is when the worst decisions are taken. That is why cooling off periods are crucial.'

One of the benefits of standing back is the time it gives to put a decision into proportion. David Normington comments,

> 'Most decisions seem difficult but then are not as difficult when you get into them. It is surprising how many people do not want to take decisions. The key thing is to weigh up the factors. Often it is important to reflect on them for 24 hours. Most of the decisions that are trouble-some are all about people in the end.'

In decisions following human tragedies a moment of standing back can be so important in ensuring the words are right and fit the emotions of the human situation. John, who was a manager in a manufacturing company, had to tell a mother that her son had died in a factory accident. He had to think on his feet, there was a strong time pressure and it was a conversation outside his comfort zone. His learning from the experience was that even when things have to be done quickly, you can make time just to reflect and decide what approach you are going to use and what words you will start off with. John also reflects that it doesn't matter how much you think in advance, something unexpected can happen. In this case after he had told the mother, he had to go and pick up her daughter from school and take her home without telling her what had happened.

The value of looking at illustrations from different areas of our lives is that the experience we gain in one area can directly affect the way we approach decisions in another area of our life. Learning to stand back and handle difficult decisions in our personal life can feed directly into how we handle decisions in a work situation. To embed this learning does mean our reflecting thoughtfully on what has been our learning in different situations.

Conviction doesn't mean always rushing in, it might mean deliberately standing back and having the belief that an individual should and can work out their own solutions. Sometimes standing back means dignified silence as we allow somebody to work out their own conclusions.

Chris Banks with his extensive experience of the food and drink industry reflects,

> 'A good manager has to maintain an element of distance in order to maintain their integrity. It is tough when you are talking to somebody about moving on: particularly when they can see no immediate hope and the person can only see the negative. Standing back is what you should do, but sometimes it is not easy when you have known somebody personally and know their background and their hopes and fears.

In one sense it is easier to make 1100 people redundant in a big organi-sation than the five people nearest to you.'

Eoin McLennan-Murray talks of the importance of standing back as a prisoner governor when incidents occur or there are riots. For him an ele-ment of detachment is an essential way of bringing objectivity into your emotions when a prison governor feels cross or let down by what has hap-pened. He comments,

> *'Standing back is most important when incidents occur or there are riots. As a commander you are kept away from the action: you don't face the heat of the emotion. You are quite removed and physically co-cooned. It becomes a game of chess and tactics. In one sense it is not difficult in these situations. It is more difficult when the action is in front of you. If a prisoner confronts you, you get the prisoner to talk it down. You are not controversial. You absorb aggression. You are the honest broker and gradually reduce the temperature of the situation.'*

Standing back is an essential ingredient of putting your convictions into context and allowing as much objectivity as possible to influence your thinking. But too much standing back can lead to not fully appreciating the emotional tensions in a situation. To counter this the prison governor, although away from the action, is receiving regular reports that illustrate the emotions as well as the facts of a situation.

Keeping calm

Keeping calm during the process of making and implementing difficult decisions is no easy matter. Calmness can come through, physical acts of breathing slowly, being conscious of living in more than one sphere of life and ensuring that the parallel world provides a source of calmness, holding firmly on to what are the ultimate goals in any situation, holding firm to the values and beliefs that are most important to you, or relying on the mutual support and encouragement of others.

John Gieve having worked in a sequence of demanding leadership roles reflects,

> *'I put a lot of energy into being calm. It helps to get better decisions. It helps to give other people space to catch their breath. I have learnt to re-flect. I keep calm by writing down the pluses and minuses to make my-self think dispassionately. I try to talk things through both internally*

and externally. I rehearse what I want to say and find it immensely helpful to do so.'

He tells of a situation when the media was pressing him very hard about what happened in a particular situation. In thinking about his response, he had to be ready for what he might have to say before a Select Committee. He wrote down carefully what he had done and rehearsed what he would say. The process of being clear in his own mind about what he was going to say in a demanding situation was such a release and renewed in him the calmness that was needed for next steps.

Many leaders are not at all sure how well they score on calmness, maybe they have reached their current positions by being constantly energetic. Justin McCracken recognises that he has mixed success on calmness. He comments,

> *'I can be seen as impatient. I do not see myself as excitable or irrational, but when I am sure I am right I have no difficulty in being courageous in progressing matters and find delays frustrating. If I feel pushed in a direction that I feel uncomfortable with I will stall to buy time to reflect. I will use this time to discuss the issue and my concerns with others to help me work through my difficulties in a calm and measured way.'*

David Normington has successfully come through times when the department of which he has been Permanent Secretary has been in the limelight. He comments,

> *'A crucial thing is keeping calm throughout the whole process and needing to steady the team. Calmness comes from experience. It is never as bad as you think. Don't allow yourself to be panicked because you have coped before.'*

Keeping calm is not an optional extra. You may think that you do not need to keep calm in order to make good decisions. But the lack of calmness in a leader can have a destructive effect right through a team. The most unfair treatment a leader can give to their followers is to be so anxious that they sap the calmness out of their followers. Therein lies the route to short-termism and ill-considered decisions. As one ex-Army leader put it, 'don't rush around or you will panic the troops'.

The importance of conversations with colleagues

Many leaders comment on the importance of talking through difficult decisions with others. It helps provide an honest second opinion and gives the leader an opportunity to articulate a line of argument to see whether it stacks up or not.

Good conversations with colleagues or partners can lead to an outcome which is more than the sum of the parts. Nick Holgate, a director general in the UK Department for Culture, Media and Sport, tells the story of working on a five-person team doing a capability review of another department. He described the teamwork as a very creative process. They were seeing objective evidence through a variety of perspectives and were asking each other whether there was a particular insight from the evidence.

Because these five people came with different perspectives there was an iterative process: one person would set off a particular idea with group dialogue following. It worked best when the five people were building their own understanding and elaborating and developing one another's contributions. It was important to use a variety of stimuli and ideas to ensure that one person's conviction was tested and developed so the overall understanding grew and enabled the team to decide what its recommendation should be. This process was both about testing out one another's intuitive reactions and about each individual drawing slightly different conclusions from the same shared analysis.

Rigorous conversations with colleagues can be such a valuable approach in testing out the significance of different factors. The conversation itself can help you stand back and keep calm. The perspective from a colleague who knows of such situations can enable a new angle to be explored or new perspective seen. Setting aside some time to talk through a difficult issue with a colleague is hardly ever wasted time provided you are open to listen and weigh up the perspective given in a measured way. If you are either too deferential to your colleague or determined to keep to your own way, come what may, then the conversation is unlikely to be as productive as it could be.

It is worth reflecting on:

- Who are the colleagues whose views I most trust?
- How best do I glean the views of those I trust most?
- Do I treat those views in an open and considered way?
- Am I likely to be too deferential or resistant to the views of particular colleagues: can I make an allowance for this potential distortion in advance?

- Do I acknowledge to my colleagues how much I appreciate conversations with them when working through difficult decisions?
- Do I give colleagues due credit when, as a result of a conversation, I have got myself into a position where I am much better able to make a difficult decision?

Mentoring

Many organisations encourage individuals to have a mentor. A business mentor is an experienced executive from the same or similar business who has direct experience of the individual's broad situation and can help them work through different concerns effectively. The distinction between a mentor and a manager is that the mentor has no line management responsibility for the individual. A mentor can provide a source of knowledge of the organisation, its political climate and the organisational politics, act as a sounding-board for ideas or help an individual think through and plan an overall career development path.

In many organisations there is a pattern of decisions that need to be made. A mentor who has been through these difficult decisions before is in an excellent place to give advice as another generation of individuals experiences a similar set of decisions. For example:

- a procurement expert who has been through difficult procurement exercises can help mentor a newly qualified specialist;
- a financial trader who has been through many oscillations in the stock market will have developed a sense of awareness about when circumstances are going to change: they can bring that sensitivity to mentoring a younger trader;
- a prison governor who has talked with many prisoners and has built up a sense of when they are being told the truth and when only partial truth, can help build up the same sensitivity in a younger prison officer;
- the leader who has led hundreds of staff will have a wealth of experience about what works or doesn't work in different situations and can mentor a new leader through challenges of leadership in a fast changing world.

A helpful question is: do I have any mentors I can draw on as I develop my capability in making difficult decisions?

Coaching

Focused coaching can play an important part in enabling individuals to make difficult decisions well. In early 2006, an independent survey was conducted of 80 individuals who are coached by members of the partnership of which I am a member. The individuals were asked about the objectives for the coaching and its outcomes. The main types of objectives were as follows:

- *business issues*: strategic priorities, business planning, major projects;
- *clarity of role:* transitional coaching into a new role, career development and preparation for subsequent roles;
- *personal awareness:* impact, leadership style, confidence, self-belief and assertiveness; and
- *interpersonal skills:* influencing skills, stakeholder management and team management and development.

Within each of these types of objectives, sharpening the process of decision-making is always present.

An external coach who has held a senior position in the private, public or voluntary sector with extensive experience of coaching people in senior roles in a variety of situations can provide that external stimulus and challenge, which can enable an individual to make difficult decisions well and become increasingly effective as a senior leader.

The benefits of one-to-one coaching with an experienced coach for individuals should be:

- deeper self-belief and confidence in tackling demanding challenges;
- greater courage in delivering change;
- a broader repertoire of approaches to solving problems;
- a clearer set of priorities;
- more focused value-added;
- better use of energy and vitality; and
- increased self-awareness and a better understanding of their impact on others.

The value of coaching work with individuals facing difficult decisions is both the strengthening of the capabilities above and the opportunity to use a coach as a sounding-board in working through the decisions themselves.

The benefits for an organisation of focused coaching with its senior leaders should include:

- a clearer vision and strategy;
- a stronger commitment from leaders to organisational goals;
- a sharper set of priorities for the organisation;
- stronger personal impact of the senior leaders internally and externally;
- more productive working relationships;
- better delivery of results; and
- the testing out of courses of action in a safe space.

This should add up to better decision-making across a whole organisation resulting from both hard edged learning in individuals and a greater emotional sensitivity and awareness of others. The success of coaching in enabling individuals to take decisions effectively depends on:

- the quality of engagement between coach and client;
- the clarity of objectives for the coaching;
- the openness to change on behalf of the individual;
- a willingness to reflect and learn;
- a willingness to experiment with taking difficult decisions and embed that new learning;
- the accuracy of external feedback;
- an ability to use self-awareness constructively;
- a recognition that coaching is a journey with the need for challenging objectives that evolve with experience; and
- support from the organisation and the boss in allowing an individual to learn through addressing and taking difficult decisions.

Coaching, if it is to be effective in enabling an individual to move up a step in their ability to take difficult decisions, must be about focused conversations in which the individual feels both strongly supported and effectively challenged and stretched. Good coaching will be both exhausting and invigorating. The long-term result will be a strong sense of purpose, a clarity about aspirations and a set of pragmatic and focused next steps in addressing difficult issues. Its overall impact on an organisation will be leaders making better decisions, with the organisation's performance improving as a consequence. (In our book *Business Coaching: achieving practical results through effective engagement* Robin Linnecar and I set out in more detail the impact of coaching, what makes a good coach, different formats for coaching and different contexts where coaching can make a significant difference.)

Mal Singh talks of the benefits of coaching for him in decision-making as a senior official in a UK government department in the following way:

'Coaching has helped me to evaluate both business and personal options. It has made me much more receptive to understanding the impact of different strategies. It has helped me recognise that people will always welcome options which create win-win outcomes. The coaching has enabled me more readily to break down complex issues into simple themes and to understand what the surrounding noise is.'

The focused use of coaching can play an important part in developing the capability to make decisions well. Key tests are:

- What is the capability I want to develop through coaching?
- How will I measure progress?
- Am I willing to see my understanding and capabilities stretched?

Awareness of pitfalls

Within the theme of conviction there are a sequences of pitfalls to watch. These include the following.

Watch resentment when others make final decisions

Watching the personal emotions can be important. When you have been making the running on a particular issue you sometimes have to accept that somebody else is going to make the decision. You cannot have your own way on everything and might need to watch any sense of resentment if another person is making the final decision. In this type of situation Archie Hughes advises,

'Set out the options and then accept the conclusions when other people are taking decisions. When my views are overturned, I need to bring practical common sense. I need to be able to rationalise the conclusion. It was important to recognise that "course correction" is part of effective leadership.'

This resentment can be particularly acute if you have been the one who previously made the decisions and now it is somebody else's responsibility. Moving yourself on into a new place where you accept that it is for somebody else to make the decisions is not easy. This may be particularly acute if you have moved sideways in an organisation and still feel a strong vested interest in a particular area. The answer is often about forcing yourself into a different type of contribution and being generous in praise to the person now making the decisions.

Watch feeling you have to do it all again
As you move up an organisation other people do the detailed work for you. It is not always easy for a leader to accept that when somebody has done the detailed work for them, they need not feel they have to do it all again! Allowing yourself to trust that the preparatory work has been done well is an important step forward. Biting back frustration and not letting it show is so important. It can also mean holding back sometimes to allow others to have the time to make their own decisions.

Watch becoming blinkered
Someone with a strong conviction can be very successful initially because of their single mindedness. But where strong conviction blanks out changes in reality success can rapidly become damaging failure.

Barbara, with a strong consultancy track record in international firms, came into a new organisation and set up a consultancy practice on change management. All the processes were good in theory. The team developed a good method but no one wanted to buy it. Instead of recognising that people did not want to buy this approach the organisation began packaging it differently. The conviction of the leader blinkered people. There was a danger of building too much on small successes. Senior people were not comfortable to admit they had made a mistake. It took a long time before people had the courage to say that a fundamental change of direction was needed and that they did not think the approach taken by Barbara was working.

Watch whether you are always in your comfort zone
There are inevitably aspects of decision-making we feel more comfortable with than others. We can hide away in the analysis bit if we are not so keen on listening to others. The following are some types of reactions from a seminar I led on making difficult decisions which illustrates how easy it is to be stuck in a comfort zone.

- I am really good at agonising: I need to tell myself when to stop agonising;
- I must allow myself to stand back and create the space to do so;
- I love to get into the detail. I must do more listening and patient standing back;
- I need to work on courage and coherence and being bolder. I like the strategic stuff: I am not a details person and need other people around me to help me with that;
- I spend too much time on the reasons that got us into a particular situation: I need to force myself to look ahead more.

Whatever our comfort zone is, being honest about it and deciding how we strengthen different aspects of our approach is a necessary step. Sometimes this is best done alone, but often it benefits from the support of others, either from within or outside the organisation of which we are part.

Watch for the hidden traps to decision-making
In their article 'The Hidden Traps in Decision-making' Hammond, Keeney and Raiffa (*Harvard Business Review*, September–October 1998) suggests that the way the human brain works can sabotage the decisions we make. This article reflects on eight psychological traps that are particularly likely to affect the way we make business decisions.

- The **anchoring trap** can lead us to give disproportionate weight to the first information we receive;
- The **status quo trap** can bias us towards maintaining the current situation even when better alternatives exist;
- The **sunk cost trap** inclines us to perpetuate mistakes of the past;
- The **confirming evidence trap** leads us to seek out information supporting an existing predeliction and to discount opposing information;
- The **framing trap** occurs when we mis-state a problem, undermining the entire decision-making process;
- The **overconfidence trap** makes us overestimate the accuracy of our forecasts;
- The **prudence trap** leads us to be overcautious when we make estimates about uncertain events;
- The **recallability trap** leads us to give undue weight to recent and dramatic events.

The authors' thrust is that awareness forewarned is forearmed. They suggest ways of handling these traps which are summarised below.
    The **anchoring trap** of giving disproportionate weight to the first information might be addressed by:

- always viewing a problem from different perspectives, e.g. trying an alternative starting point;
- thinking about the problem on your own before consulting others in order to avoid being anchored by their ideas;
- being open-minded and seeking information and opinions from a variety of people to widen your frame of reference;
- being careful to avoid anchoring your advisers from whom you solicit the information and counsel;
- avoiding being anchored by the other party's initial proposition.

Possible ways to avoid the **status quo trap** might be:

- always remind yourself of your objectives and examine how they will be served by the status quo;
- never think of the status quo as your only option;
- ask yourself whether you would choose the status quo option if in fact it weren't the status quo;
- avoid exaggerating the effort or cost involved in switching from the status quo;
- remember that the desirability of the status quo will change over time: always evaluate alternatives in terms of the future as well as the present.

Some of the ways of addressing the **sunk cost trap** might be:

- seek out and listen carefully to the views of people who were uninvolved in the earlier decisions and who are unlikely to be committed to them;
- examine why admitting to an earlier mistake distresses you. What are the emotional reasons? Is it wounded self-esteem? Is it sometimes worth remembering that good decisions can have bad consequences through no fault of the original decision maker?
- be on the lookout for the influence or cost biases in the decisions and recommendations by your staff;
- don't cultivate a failure-fearing culture that leads people to perpetuate their mistakes.

With the **confirming evidence trap** we have to face up to the tendency to subconsciously decide what we want to do before we figure out what we really want to do. A related distortion is our inclination to be more engaged by things we like than by things we dislike. Ways of addressing the confirming evidence trap involve:

- always checking to see whether you are examining all the evidence with equal vigour;
- getting somebody you respect to play devil's advocate to argue against the decision you are contemplating or build the counter arguments yourself;
- be honest with yourself about your motives,. Are you looking for evidence to make a smart choice or for evidence to support your previous decision?
- in seeking the advice of others don't ask leading questions that invite confirming evidence.

The **framing trap** is potentially the most dangerous one. The first step in making a decision is to frame the question. If the question is framed wrongly the framing trap can establish the status quo or introduce an anchor that isn't going to work. Approaches that can be used to limit the framing problem include:

- not automatically accepting the initial frame but always trying to re-frame the problem in various ways and looking for distortions caused by the frame;
- posing problems in a neutral, redundant way that combines gains and losses or embraces different reference points;
- thinking hard throughout the decision-making process about the framing of the problem. When others recommend decisions examine the way they have framed the problem.

The **recallability trap** is about the way we frequently base our predictions about future events on our memory of past events. For example we can exaggerate the probability of rare but catastrophic occurrences because they get disproportionate attention in the media. The authors suggest the best way to avoid the estimating and forecasting trap is to have a very disciplined approach to making forecasts and judging probabilities. Too much emphasis on worst case analysis can distort decision-making. Worst case analysis can add enormous costs with limited practical benefits.

The authors conclude that the best way of addressing these hidden traps in decision-making is through awareness of these dangers. Their approach is 'forewarned is forearmed' whereby even if you cannot eradicate the distortions ingrained into the way our minds work, we can build in tests and disciplines that will expose these distortions in our thinking before they become errors in judgement. Being ready for and avoiding these psychological traps can then enable us to improve significantly the quality of our decision-making.

Next steps

The elements of conviction set out in this chapter can provide both profound guiding principles and good sense, but can also lead to blinkeredness, egg-headedness, randomness and bizarre decisions. The elements of conviction have to be treated with considerable caution and respect, but are essential elements in making difficult decisions.

It might be worth reflecting on:

- What part does conviction play in the way you make decisions?
- How much is your reliance on intuition and past experience, a reliable guide or source of vulnerability?
- How big a part do your values play in decision-making, are they consistent with the way you want to make decisions happen?
- How do you want to further develop your capability in using conviction to good effect in decision-making?

Chapter 4

Courage

What is the place of courage in taking forward difficult decisions? Lewis Carroll included these wonderful words in 'Through the Looking Glass', *'I am brave generally'*, he went on in a low voice, *'only today I happen to have a headache!'*.

Does courage enable us to do good things well or does it mean we make ill judged decisions in a blinkered and insensitive way? Courage does not come from a bloated sense of our own importance or a quick shot of whisky. True courage is something much more deep seated and is about:

- being comfortable with our own values;
- addressing our fears;
- being willing to be bold when we feel strongly about an issue;
- knowing what happens if we are courageous and willing to take bold steps;
- recognising and enjoying the courage of others and learning from their approaches.

Maybe courage is also about:

- always being curious;
- asking the right questions and probing;
- identifying risks and being clear how significant they are and thinking clearly about what the right next steps might be;
- not going with the flow sometimes when key facts are being ignored or misinterpreted; and
- taking a stand if a course of action is clearly unfair and counterproductive in its treatment of individuals.

But courage can have its limits. The ethics professor, Jack Mahoney, talks about how our courage can be defective in two ways, one by having too little courage, when we are overwhelmed by our fears; and the other by having too much of it, when courage becomes recklessness and we pay no regard to dangers and difficulties. He says that we do not call people courageous when they take stupid risks with their cars: we call them reckless drivers. He links together courage and caution when solving a problem that depends not just on courage but on taking due thought and care in one's actions.

This chapter looks at the importance of courage through the three dimensions of action, reflection and ensuring progress as illustrated in Figure 4.1 below.

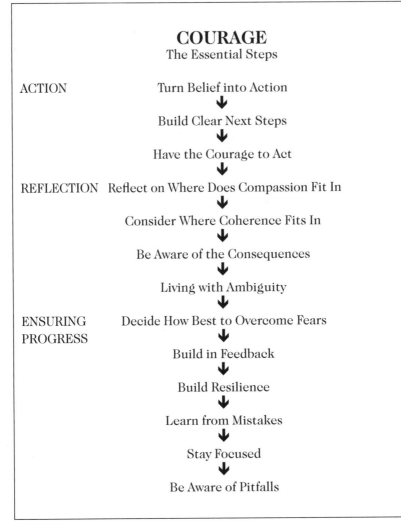

Figure 4.1   Courage: the essential steps

Action

This covers turning belief into action, building clear next steps and having the courage to act.

Turn belief into action

Courage doesn't just happen; it grows over a period. John Gieve talks of courage being about confidence and using experience and authority to put a limit on what you say and when. When he became Permanent Secretary at the Home Office he faced a sequence of difficult issues following events such as the destruction of the World Trade Towers in New York in September 2001. He talks of the resilience needed to deal with difficult decisions. He says that in these circumstances,

'You grow into it. You develop your abilities. You develop a better sense of perspective over time. The development of resilience is important. That is the capability to keep a sense of perspective and think clearly. You need to be able to live with the fact that you can't avoid the risk of failure and wrong decisions; that you have to back people as well as your own judgements and to delegate.'

For Justin McCracken courage flowed from conviction. For him the danger time is when he does not have a conviction about next steps. He talks of the toughest part of the process being getting to the conviction stage aligning 'mind and belly'. Once his conviction is clear the courage flows. He says,

'I will often have a clear view at the start which will need to be tested. But that is different to having a conviction. A conviction will grow over time as I work through an issue and will give me the courage and calmness I need to turn belief into action.'

Chris Banks expresses a caution about an emphasis on courage. He isn't convinced that it always fits well into the process of making a decision. For him it all depends on the scale of the decision and how the decision is going to be taken forward. For Chris, being over-courageous is not always a good thing as it can blur the capacity to look for unintended consequences. If you are making a big decision such as on redundancy you need to think carefully about the knock-on consequences on others and be very conscious about the potentially detrimental effects of a decision. Then you can make a decision clearly without feeling you have to be over courageous about it.

A group of individuals I talked with about courage were very clear about what it meant for them in difficult situations. Some of their perspectives were:

- courage is intimately linked to confidence and inner strength;
- courage is not being swayed by the emotional reactions of others;
- courage is about building resilience to reduce the risk of disappointment;
- it is about effective preparation and consistency so there is a purposefulness that is not easily undermined.

While for many, thinking about courage and how they turn belief into action is a necessary step, for many leaders courage is not something that they think about separately. Archie Hughes comments,

> *'On courage I very rarely think about it in advance. But when I have come in with a big picture plan, then in retrospect some may say I have been courageous. While I am willing to be bold I do not gamble on decisions. I always take big decisions within a firm frame of reference. It is important to have the courage of your convictions, but they must be rooted in a firm frame of reference.'*

Turning belief into action: a case study

Peter Collis is the chief executive of the Land Registry. Because of the adoption of radical changes in e-technology such as e-conveyancing there was going to be a reduction from 8000 employees to 5000. A blueprint was produced about what the organisation would look like in the future. The consequence of reduced numbers of staff was going to be excess office space. Leases in Harrow and York were to run out in the next few years. In five cities there were two offices when there only needed to be one.

Decisions about next steps in terms of office space were not intellectually hard. The announcements were not difficult to draft. People could see it coming. Senior management had been signposting the necessity for change over a period. Peter talks about the 'hardest thing' being standing up in front of people saying, 'This is what we are going to do'. The difficult aspects were not the intellectual elements of the decision but the emotional dimension.

There was extensive consultation and careful listening. The consultation took longer than anticipated. Dealing with the frustration of staff was important. For many, the frustration was about their preference for an early decision because of commitments that they needed to make, for example about school education. Peter commented,

'The hard bits were about the announcement itself and dealing with the consequences. As I talked with people in the organisation about the decision I was very open about the logic of the need to close offices but also open about my own emotions and frustrations.'

For Peter the need to close offices was balanced with an understanding of the emotions and frustrations of those affected. It meant listening to them hard through consultation but then being clear about the logic of the final decision. It was about being open in sharing his own frustrations but also honest in not letting those frustrations dilute the necessity of firm action.

Build clear next steps

Building next steps is not about rushing into a decision. Sometimes it is moving quite slowly. Sometimes it is about the courage to hold back. Pete Worrall comments, from his experience as a chief executive in a European business,

> 'Courage is most important when you are under pressure in negotiation. The adrenalin drive can lead to failure. Success may be about holding back. Reaching a deal must not be success at any cost. I was close to a deal recently involving millions of Euros and I stopped the negotiation.'

For Pete, courage at this point meant stopping the negotiation when there was almost a remorseless push to reach a conclusion. For him, a period of stepping back was important before a final decision was taken. He said,

> 'The key issue is having the courage sometimes to stop. When you then move forward and take hard decisions things sometimes fall into place. You have a silver bullet to use occasionally: you must use it well. It can be the last chance to reposition or save a deal.'

For Pete, building next steps also involves being careful not to back anyone into a corner or apply a nuclear option unless you are clear that you can use it. One of the biggest derailers to measured courage can come when you feel annoyed with individuals: the danger then is irrational decisions based on emotional reactions rather than a steady focus based on both clarity and conviction.

John Gieve echoes some of the same sentiments about not rushing to a conclusion:

> 'One of my rules is not to be pressured into taking decisions too quickly. For example there can be huge pressure in government to respond to press stories to meet their schedules. It can be important not to say anything until you have complete clarity on the facts. The real story behind many so-called "cover ups" is that people have rushed into statements before they have had time to check the facts.'

He quotes an example of how every two hours he was being chased for an answer about what should be sent to a journalist but did not give an answer until 6 o'clock when he was clear about the facts. For John there was a balance between sometimes not taking decisions too quickly and on other occasions ensuring that he stayed ahead of the game.

Building new steps can be about how you take people with you effectively, mindful of their likely reaction to situations. Rosalyn holds a senior position in a body at arms length to government. She was told by her interlocutor in a government department that an item was going to be included within a forthcoming White Paper which her chief executive would find difficult. Her dilemma was if she told the chief executive immediately there would be an emotive and possibly counterproductive reaction, but was she being dishonest if she didn't relay the information straightaway?

Rosalyn decided not to rush things, she didn't fire off an immediate e-mail, She waited for an opportunity to talk with her chief executive in a reflective way about this issue and together they arrived at a rational set of next steps. For Rosalyn this was an important example of understanding in advance somebody's likely reaction if information is presented in a particular way. Far better to create a situation where there can be careful and measured discussion.

Building next steps is often about drawing on previous experience. Once a difficult situation has been handled well it is often more straightforward handling a similar situation in the future.

A crucial element of building next steps is matching individual accountability with ownership across an organisation. Mel Zuydam has held finance director posts in both the private and public sectors. He comments on the need for a combination of the accountability of the individual leaders while not taking decisions on your own. He described this balance as,

> *'Putting all the information on the wall and getting people to own and make decisions. It is about ensuring that any organisation has clear ownership at senior levels about decisions so that decisions are not just taken forward in an isolated way but are part of a wider plan of intent.'*

For Mel it is important there is good support for people making decisions and taking them forward so that once a decision is made there is a corporate intent to make it happen.

Have the courage to act

Many leaders will look back and recognise occasions when they should have acted earlier. When Suma Chakrabarti became Permanent Secretary at the UK Department for International Development he wanted to reshape the policy function. He set up a project team but talks of making the following mistakes,

'I let it drag on too long and had never signalled the red lines, I had not generated a sense of urgency, the project team thought that whatever they came up with I would accept as the right answer, I didn't engage as deeply as I should have done, and I wanted to be seen to be good to the individual leading the project.'

In terms of lessons that Suma drew from this experience he said,

'I had put some conviction in at an early stage but not enough. My involvement was a bit random. I didn't communicate what I thought effectively. I left the initiative too much to one person.'

Leigh Lewis talks of the lessons he has learnt about the courage to act. He comments,

'When there are difficult decisions to communicate about somebody moving on, you always do it yourself. You do it straight. You offer the maximum amount of personal support.'

We all enjoy 'armchair courage' especially when supporting a favoured sporting team. But the courage to act involves putting ourselves 'on the line' and taking full responsibility for our choices. There is that apprehension, and sometimes the sense of exhilaration, as we hold our nose and jump into the water.

Reflection

Reflection embraces the themes of: the place of compassion, where coherence fits in, the awareness of consequences and living with ambiguity.

Reflect where compassion fits in

Is compassion a necessary part of decision-making or does it get in the way of reaching objective conclusions? Compassion is a recognition of individual humanity when mistakes are made and individuals are rarely entirely consistent. But too much compassion can dilute clarity of purpose and mean that excessive kindness to one person can mean gross unfairness for others.

Many leaders see the importance of compassion as a element of decision-making. Nicky Munroe is clear that there is a role for compassion in successful and healthy organisations. She comments,

'You cannot create respect in an organisation if you don't take compassion into account in some decisions. That doesn't mean shrinking from tough action. It does mean thinking at the same time about doing it right, keeping people on side and helping the organisation move on quickly.'

Her argument is that where an organisation has used compassion sensitively in decision-making, the impact will be to increase the commitment of members of the organisation.

Rosemary, a senior project manager, talks of a decision she had to make recently in a discipline case. One of her staff had been discovered fiddling his flexitime. There had been difficult domestic situations at home but it was not acceptable behaviour. Dismissal would have been perfectly legitimate but she decided to demote the individual with a condition that he could not be promoted back within two years which meant the individual kept his job. Rosemary was comfortable with the outcome of the process, for her it was an example of balancing compassion with clarity. Because the individual had deliberately breached the rules there needed to be clarity about the penalty they were going to suffer. There was compassion because of the difficult family circumstances and the emotional turmoil the individual was going through. The effect was that the individual felt relieved and shocked, with the result being a more disciplined work pattern. The lesson had been learnt and compassion had worked.

Linda Freestone, an Immigration Judge, talks of the importance of compassion in the decisions she takes. As a judge you are weighing up the facts very carefully but it is valid to consider the impact on people of the judgements you make. For her, compassion is relevant to the way people are treated in the hearing room and in delivering difficult decisions both written and orally.

Chris Banks talks of the key issue of whether you are making decisions objectively and then executing them compassionately, or whether you are making compassion part of the decision. He comments,

'One way of addressing this dilemma when talking to people you are going to have to make redundant is to say that you will take forward that action in as thoughtful a way as possible and then follow it up practically, consistent with the commitments you made.'

His view is that you cannot take compassion out of decision-making completely: it is more honest to recognise that it will be an element within decisions. But understanding the influence of compassion upon you is important.

Decisions are multilayered. There is the decision about whether to reduce the number of jobs and then a decision about how individuals leave
the business with dignity. Compassion is unlikely to be relevant to the first
layer but is likely to be relevant to the second layer.

Although Archie Hughes has in different jobs made significant numbers
of people redundant he is clear that compassion has a part to play.

> *'You have to be compassionate and care about people. I had to make
> 2000 people redundant. There was a clarity about the decisions which
> resulted from commercial necessity and ministerial decisions. Clarity
> of purpose was important. There had to be conviction to see it through
> where stamina has been crucial. But as the decisions are taken forward
> you have to take account of the environment and the wider context.
> You have to understand how people are feeling and care about the con-
> sequences of your decisions.'*

Eoin McLennan-Murray is conscious of balancing compassion and clarity as a prison governor when considering the option of Home Detention
Curfew for a prisoner. The question is what circumstances is it agreed to,
particularly when a second offence has been involved. Eion talks of situations when there has been a breach of trust with the choice of bringing in
the discipline code or using different means to try to make somebody feel
ashamed and therefore change their approach. For Eion,

> *'The compassion dimension is relevant in terms of building a picture of
> when somebody is being genuine and when their human nature makes
> it very difficult for them to change. Do you always punish somebody
> who has got it wrong? Where does compassion play a role in these cir-
> cumstances? If somebody is scheming it is a very different situation
> than when people make genuine mistakes.'*

Other leaders see less scope for compassion. Martin Oakley who has a
senior regulatory role within an international financial business talks of
the importance of being clinical in making decisions. On issues of regulatory compliance his perspective is, there has either been a breach or not.
Sometimes he thinks he takes too much notice of compassion. He reflects,

> *'Sometimes reflecting on compassion makes the decision more itchy
> than it should be. It slows you down. It sometimes means you creep
> towards a decision.'*

Justin McCracken, drawing on his experience in the health and safety world, does not see compassion as having a primary role in decision-making. Too much compassion can take you to too soft an option. But he is clear that compassion is important in managing the consequences. He comments,

> *'It is not so important that the decision maker is able to live with the consequences (that comes from following one's conscience). What is important is that the consequences of tough decisions are managed in a compassionate way, so that those who are inevitably affected are treated with respect and helped to find a positive way forward for themselves.'*

This does involve a decision maker thinking carefully about the consequences of their action and supporting an individual when an individual's self-esteem is damaged.

Stephen Timms drawing from his experience as a government minister sees compassion as both a sensitisor and a risk. He sees it as an important indicator but recognises that it can be a distortion. He talks of the danger of being more compassionate to people like yourself than to people who are different to you.

Various leaders have commented about how their level of compassion has varied over time. Hazel talks about how in previous jobs compassion had burnt out her soul. Difficult decisions had meant that compassion no longer existed. She was conscious that she needed to reinvent some compassion sometimes. She said the turning point was when somebody began to talk about the emotional consequences for spina bifida babies if no action was taken.

The relevance of compassion is inevitably a sensitive issue. But without any sense of compassion or humanity our decision-making can become mechanical and brutal. Relevant questions might be:

- Is compassion influencing my approach?
- Is compassion distorting my perspective or allowing me to see an issue from a different perspective?
- If I exercise compassion is it being unfair on others?
- Is my exercising of compassion likely to lead to a better long-term outcome?
- Is compassion an excuse for not making a difficult decision?
- Is applying compassion living out or distorting my values in this instance?

Consider where coherence fits in

A potential test for any decision is how coherent is it when looked at in relation to other parallel decisions. For some this is a primary test. For a decision maker working in regulatory compliance coherence is a particularly important measure. For a judge the coherence between different decisions is important if a judgement is to be readily explicable.

But coherence can become a cause of rigidity. A key consideration is the balance between coherence and adaptability to particular circumstances. John Gieve comments,

> *'You need fixed points or you get blown away. You are always being asked to respond to the unwanted or unexpected, therefore coherence is an operational necessity. But you must be willing to be flexible.'*

Leigh Lewis echoes some of the same concerns about the importance of flexibility, he is not sure about the importance of coherence and regards it as double-edged. His perspective is that you have to look at precedents but you do not necessarily have to stick to precedent. He comments, *'I do question when people say that the past has enormous implications.'* For Leigh each decision needs to be taken on its merits having considered precedents while not rigidly applying a test of consistency with previous decisions. For him every situation is different with a range of factors needing to be weighed up carefully.

Stephen Timms as a government minister is clear that he expects coherence to be provided by officials when they give advice. But for him, *'Coherence is a filter, an important test that should not be a driver.'*

Perhaps the elements of the coherence test in thinking through a decision can be expressed as:

- To what extent are there precedents and how binding are they?
- Are there previous decisions which provide an important essential framework affecting this decision?
- To what extent is this situation different to previous situations?
- Am I being too bound by precedent?
- How do I explain the difference between this decision and previous decisions to a neutral questioner?

Be aware of the consequences

Most decisions have knock-on consequences. In one sense they are irrelevant as a decision needs to be taken on the merits of the case. But ignoring the consequences can turn a minor decision into a catastrophe. When might a decision take someone 'over the edge'? When might one small decision set off a whole chain of controversial next steps? Some decisions are irreversible and therefore have much more severe consequences than others.

Findlay Scott, the chief executive of the General Medical Council, talks of a technique he recommends when making a difficult decision. You 'make' the decision in your mind but first of all put it in a drawer without announcing it. You will then be mulling over the arguments in your mind. Having 'made' the decision the consequences will become much clearer and enable you to reassess whether the decision is the right one.

Abdul had produced a report which was inevitably going to be controversial within his organisation. At what stage did he show it to one of the board members? He was very open in developing his ideas with the chief executive, but knew that if he shared his thoughts with one of the board members there would be an immediate attempt to block his proposals. So he was cagey with that board member until he had built a stronger consensus about next steps. Abdul explained this approach of sounding out people first who could view the issue dispassionately as a guiding instinct based on experience. It was a matter of thinking issues through with people who would be constructive before making a final decision. He knew that he needed to address the issue with this particular board member but at a time and context of his choosing.

Julian Duxfield, an HR specialist, talks of the most difficult decisions on staff being whether you let somebody go or not. As an HR director with experience in both the public and private sectors he is focused primarily on the consequences for the organisation. He comments,

> 'You need to collect as much information as you can but you must not let the collection of evidence paralyse you. You need to get significant feedback but not too much. Then you need to take a step back and look at the consequences. It may be better to develop the person you know than go for somebody you don't know.'

Linda Freestone, as an Immigration Judge, looks at consequences from a different perspective. She is very conscious of the consequences of some of her decisions as a judge for the individual. As a District Judge some of the major decisions she took meant a custodial sentence with the consequences, intended and unintended, for an individual that often result from prison life. On other occasions, sitting as an Immigration Judge, she is very conscious that she is sending somebody back to their home country, which can have implications for their personal safety and will certainly affect their economic and family well being.

Looking at the consequences is a valid test in any decision. Key questions might be:

- Have the implications of each option been explored fully?
- Are the consequences of a favoured decision clear for the organisation, the stakeholders and the individual?
- To what extent are the consequences reversible, is that a relevant consideration?
- Are the likely consequences consistent with the significance of the initial decision?
- Does looking at the consequences lead you to want to revisit the decision or not?
- Having thought through the consequences do you remain convinced about the validity of the initial decision?

Living with ambiguity

Learning to live with ambiguity can be a great skill and knowing when a decision will make itself is critical. Living with ambiguity can be about:

- living with conflicting priorities;
- acknowledging there are a variety of perspectives from key stakeholders;
- recognising the time is not yet right for a decision because of a particular fixed perspective;
- awaiting the arrival of new data; and
- awaiting changes in the external market.

The best action may be no action. It might be holding back from making a decision until there is greater clarity or you feel confident that now is the right time to make a decision.

Ensuring progress

The ingredients of ensuring progress include deciding how best to overcome your fears, building in feedback and resilience, learning from mistakes, staying focused and being aware of pitfalls.

Decide how best to overcome fears

The best of decision makers will always have a sense of apprehension. It is rare for a good leader to be insensitive to their own apprehensions and sometimes fear. The apprehension may result from the uncertainties in a situation as well as a lack of self-belief about whether you have got the decision right. For many leaders the key ingredient is how they manage ambiguity and uncertainty. It may well mean dealing with the conflict and self-doubt internally before deciding how to act.

Nicky Munroe talks of coping with moments of self-doubt. She says,

> *'Exposing to people that you may have a black period is never easy. The issue is how you cope with moments of self-doubt. How will you cope in a period when you do not know the outcome. It is the dark night of the soul that can be a problem. You feel that people are trying to undermine you. You are feeling unconfident and yet you know that a decision has to be taken. Many contemporary and historical leaders we think of as hugely confident, have experienced and overcome these doubts, just as some of our best actors still suffer from stage fright before dazzling us in performance.'*

Archie Hughes talks of the importance of keeping fresh so that any fear in making a decision is minimised. Sometimes, while doing nothing is the correct thing, he has to be very clear with himself that this is the right decision. It is that delicate balance between keeping fresh with new ideas and then reflecting before rushing to take forward new ideas. It is being self-aware enough to recognise that the desire to take quick action can be an attempt to suppress rather than address the question of whether a decision does need to be made at that point.

Leaders often talk about their apprehension in giving individuals difficult messages. But the consistent experience is that when a difficult message has been given thoughtfully and carefully the response is often, 'thank you for being so straightforward'.

If fears surface when difficult decisions have to be made, ways of addressing the fears can include:

- writing them down and scoring them on a scale of 1 to 10, where 1 is illusory and 10 is highly likely;
- trying to understand the causes of the fear;
- aiming to be as rational as possible in the way you respond;
- limiting the size of the fear and being as specific as possible about its consequences; and
- reflecting on the consequence of each fear at its worst.

Build in feedback

Seeing ourselves as others see us can be the first step in changing our approach and behaviour. I will often accompany senior leaders as they visit different groups of people, give presentations or chair meetings. Recently I spent a day with George, a deputy chief executive collecting feedback from a range of different individuals about how the deputy chief executive came over. The message was in many ways very reassuring as he was clearly trusted and respected and built rapport very quickly. In other respects there were small points of possible change in his approach which would make a huge impact.

George needed to be clearer about the purpose of the meetings and about their conclusions. His natural inclination was to move on quickly to the next meeting: he needed the courage to slow down and be absolutely clear that the conclusions of the meeting had been stated and understood and were not just in his own head. The danger was that if he was not explicit in his conclusions people would read more than he intended into his body language and his passing comments and create a set of instructions from informal comments.

When George was given this feedback at lunchtime he immediately responded in a positive way. During the afternoon he was exemplary in the clear way he introduced and concluded meetings. The effect was much greater clarity, with those participating in the meetings having a stronger understanding of next steps. A receptive deputy chief executive had immediately internalised the feedback and adapted his approach to excellent effect.

Giving feedback often requires a dose of courage. Henry recounts an occasion when the chief executive had asked if some unsolicited feedback he had received was right. Henry decided to be very clear in his comment back and said that the feedback was right – he was not visible enough in one part of the organisation. He went on to suggest some low risk ways in which his profile might be raised. Judging from the body language this did not go down too well with the chief executive and the conversation moved on. But a few days later the chief executive said to Henry he was glad that he had made this comment, and he was reflecting on it. The courage to give honest feedback can have positive consequences, normally for the best.

Questions to ask yourself can include:

- How open am I to feedback?
- Can I respond to feedback in a way that is discerning and not defensive?
- Am I willing to give feedback in a constructive and honest way?
- How open am I to work with someone constructively after having given them clear feedback?

Build resilience

Courage is not only a matter of looking forward and taking decisions. Courage is also about building resilience to be able to respond to adverse situations. Building resilience reduces the risk of disappointment and the ability to hold back and not always give an instinctive response.

Resilience is recognising that sometimes circumstances go your way and sometimes they don't. When you are being courageous in pushing the boundaries on a particular issue you have to be conscious about whether you are 'putting all your eggs in one basket'. Leigh Lewis talks wisely that,

> *'In terms of courage you have got to know there is another place to go. I will always do this job as well as I can but if in the end my best isn't good enough so be it. You have to have the inner surety and not be worried about whether your boss will think better or worse of you.'*

The key to resilience is grounded self-belief and a strong sense of self-worth coupled with a strong sense of humility and willingness to learn from others.

Some practical reflections are:

- How resilient are you on a score of 1 (not resilient) to 10 (highly resilient)?
- What is it about your character or values that gives you your resilience?
- In what circumstances do you feel most resilient, and in what circumstances least resilient. What lessons can you draw from this comparison?
- In what ways can you build up your sources of resilience and how will you know that you are being successful in that?
- What is the right next step in developing that resilience?

Learn from mistakes

Courage does not mean ignoring mistakes. Learning from mistakes is a crucial part of our journey as a leader. As an executive coach when I work with individual leaders I draw far more on my failures than my successes from my earlier work as a director general.

Eoin McLennan-Murray from his perspective as a prison governor talks of the importance of strength of character and a strong belief in what you are doing, but also a willingness to recognise that you do make mistakes. He comments,

> *'Sometimes evidence is given to you and you have to make a difficult decision. When drugs were found in one of the loos the circumstantial*

evidence pointed to one person. I pushed him but he kept saying he was innocent. I had to make a decision and he went back from the rehabilitation prison to his original prison. A few days later someone came to see me and said if another person owned up to placing the drugs, could the previous guy be allowed back to the rehabilitation prison. I said yes. A few minutes later somebody sheepishly entered my room and said it was their responsibility for placing the drugs in the loo. The dilemma then was what decision to take in respect of these two people. The innocent guy returned to the rehabilitation prison, although the quality of my relationship with him was never quite the same. The individual who had admitted to placing the drugs went back to his original prison.'

Eoin was reflective about these decisions. He had weighed up the initial evidence carefully but had made the wrong decision initially. When there was new evidence he needed to be open-minded enough to reverse the decision.

Stay focused

Staying focused is about not letting others undermine you when the going gets tricky. It also requires enough self-awareness so clear focus does not become blind obstinacy. The framework of 'Vision, Values, Value-added and Vitality' can help keep the necessary trajectory (set out further in my book *The Four Vs of Leadership: vision, values, value-added and vitality*, Capstone 2006).Why these four elements?

- **vision:** this is about being clear what are the most important outcomes and not being deterred from striving towards these outcomes. Clarity of vision may mean looking at the outcomes from different angles while always keeping them in focus;
- **values:** this theme provides the underpinning for maintaining a strong focus. Without a clear values base there will be no coherence as a team aims to deliver its vision;
- **value-added:** the relentless asking of the question about how best to add value is essential to keeping an unwavering focus. As circumstances change so will the most effective way of adding value. Without posing this question contributions will become fossilised and in danger of becoming irrelevant;
- **vitality:** essential to any enterprise that is delivering difficult outcomes is keeping the energy of all the players high. Staying focused is about keeping your vitality at a high level while all around are losing theirs.

Be aware of pitfalls

Some of the key pitfalls are:

- being overly courageous and foolhardy;
- being indecisive and caught in the headlights;
- courageously rushing in entirely the wrong direction; and
- being so focused on building up your own courage that you are blinkered to the views of others.

Part of overcoming the pitfalls is the ability to weigh up the evidence and then decide and not look back. Archie Hughes comments, *'Never agonise over decisions: be as clear as you can but when you have made the decision move on.'*

Being over-courageous and foolhardy

Sometimes the reaction to the need for a difficult decision is to take a quick decision which meets the courageous test but could well turn out to be counterproductive. It is not always straightforward to distinguish between decisiveness and foolhardiness. Past experience in the view of colleagues and friends can help. The key test is whether there is a calmness as we take a decision. What is often associated with foolhardy decisions is a sense of overexcitement and bravado. So, standing back for a moment can help provide a check on whether a decision is wise or foolhardy.

Being indecisive and caught in the headlights

Indecision can 'gnaw at our soul' and sap our energy. Indecision can feed on itself so we become completely unable to think afresh or move. When we are caught in the headlights it might be timely to move to one side and deliberately look at a problem from a different angle so that any blinding light illuminates rather than obscures.

Recognising the fact of when we are caught in the headlights is important. It is when our brain keeps going round and round in circles and we make no progress that we need to move aside, get out of the full beam and come at an issue from a completely different perspective.

Courageously rushing in entirely the wrong direction

Sometimes we are so clear about the right approach that we do not consult others or we only consult those whom we know will agree with us. What do we do when the first seeds of doubt surface? Admitting we are wrong can be painful and humiliating but sometimes it is essential and unavoidable. It can give such a feeling of release when we admit an error, reposition ourselves and move on.

Being so focused on building up our own courage that we are blinkered to the views of others

If courage does not come easily and we have to build ourselves up in order to be able to make a difficult decision we can easily become blinkered to the views of others. What might be needed is a willingness to stand outside ourselves and keep looking at difficult decisions from a variety of perspectives rather than thinking that we have all the answers. There can always be the opportunity to learn from others.

Next steps

Courage is that elusive, precious quality that turns thought into action. At its best it is clear, purposeful, measured and value driven with an awareness of consequences and a willingness to learn from mistakes. It includes both reflection and action that ensures progress.

It might be worth reflecting on:

- Where does courage fit into the way you make and take forward decisions?
- Is your natural tendency to be over-courageous and foolhardy, or timid and lacking in boldness? How best can you redress that balance?
- In what forthcoming situations can you demonstrate the degree of courage that is most important to you?
- How best can you develop those reserves of courage that are needed for decisions you know you are going to have to take?

Chapter 5

Communication

Effective communication is essential in any decision-making process. Good communication is not just the effective communication of the outcome, it is looking at the process from start to finish beginning with listening, building partnership, effective engagement, building consensus and persuasion that creates a win-win situation, before reaching a point of decision.

In any decision-making process a key initial step is understanding the context and being seen to understand the perspective of others. Effective communication of the outcome is one of the last steps, although reflection throughout the process on how a decision is going to be communicated is an invaluable test in looking at the potential realism of a particular decision. This chapter looks at the whole process of communication from start to finish.

Figure 5.1 on the next page sets out a sequence of essential steps for effective communication grouped within the three key stages of building understanding, building agreement and taking action.

Building understanding

Essential elements in building understanding include, listening, building partnerships and ensuring effective engagement.

Keep listening

Francis de Sales, a French Roman Catholic Bishop in the early 17th century, wrote, 'Half-an-hour's listening is essential except when you are very busy. Then a full hour is needed.' Ann Long in her influential book *Listening* sets out six dimensions which make up a good listener's offering and skill:

1   **Respect:** giving value to the other person.
2   **Genuineness:** being open and not play-acting at listening.
3   **Empathy:** which is about seeing the world through another person's eyes.
4   **Concreteness:** helping an individual to avoid vacantness and be specific.
5   **Confrontation:** which is not about trying to catch somebody out but is about firmly and carefully enabling a person to become aware of the discrepancies in their thinking.
6   **Immediacy:** which is about being fully aware of how you are being experienced as a listener.

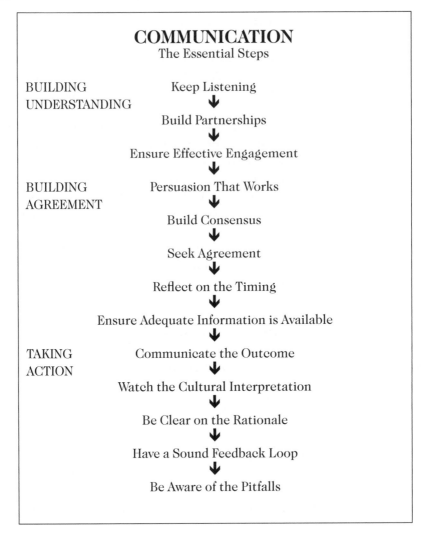

Figure 5.1 Communication: The essential steps

Juliet Erickson in her book on *The Art of Persuasion* talks of the following as good practice in listening:

- **Validate:** affirming that you have understood what somebody is saying.
- **Pause:** allowing somebody to think and give a more considered answer.

- **Ask one question at a time:** not deluging somebody with a sequence of questions.
- **Summarise:** which demonstrates that listening has happened and moves into next steps.

Stephen Timms is very conscious that communication can kill or make next steps. As Pensions Minister it became clear that the levy to fund the Pension Protection Fund would need to be a good deal higher than the initial estimate on which those who would be paying it had been consulted. Preparing people to accept the higher figure needed genuine listening and incorporating their comments into the final proposals. It was a well-planned process of listening and shaping in order to get to the point where there was an acceptance of the need for a higher levy figure. For Stephen, listening effectively was a crucial first step before a difficult decision could be accepted.

Part of listening is 'keeping an ear to the ground'. Effective listening involves the use of both formal consultation machinery and informal approaches. The observation from a junior member of staff spoken in the corridor about whether something is working or not can be an invaluable indicator. Important questions might be:

- What is the grapevine saying about what is working or not working?
- What forewarnings about difficulties are coming out from the grapevine?
- If you asked a member of staff what is their main fear about a particular issue what would they say?
- What is the office gossip about the likely outcome of a decision?
- Would the office gossip be in support of a particular decision or not?

Any board or senior team needs clarity of vision and purpose. But if there is no sense of involvement from staff or stakeholders then there is unlikely to be effective buy-in to decisions. Any board or senior team needs to be clear how it is going to listen to staff, stakeholders and customers and how it is going to demonstrate that it is listening to them.

Build partnerships

Building a strong sense of partnership is a common theme when talking to successful leaders. Justin McCracken draws from his experience as a regional director at the Environment Agency where he went out of his way to talk to those opposed to particular schemes. He comments,

'Communication is a two-way process. It is important that I receive as much as I give. Listening and being listened to are crucial. I recall a situation when a protester said to me "Your officers are not corrupt, but they drink coffee with the managers in the company and they do not drink coffee with me." It was his perception that the Environment Agency were not giving equal weight to both sides of the argument. What has stuck with me is the need both to listen to all sides of the argument, and to show that I am doing so. It was also important to adjust the communication approach to different audiences using a mixture of styles and looking at what is fit for purpose. Little things were important such as holding public enquiries at a location accessible to people and not in a far off city.'

Archie Hughes talks of the importance of 'pre-positioning' which is a process of talking to people well in advance and getting people onside to talk through the consequences of particular decisions. His view is that when you have many stakeholders who can support or derail a project, you have to be build partnerships with them starting off with a shared perspective about the problem and then moving into the necessity for change and then the potential outcomes of different next steps.

Pete Worrall from his experience as a chief executive is clear that the most important ingredient in building a team is to create a situation where there is a strong sense of partnership. He says,

'Making good decisions is about credibility and relationships and not just technical skills. It is turning data into information, and information into real useful intelligence, piecing together information like a jigsaw puzzle.'

He sees a strong sense of partnership as a key ingredient in moving to effective decisions especially when they are controversial and far reaching.

Partnership may not just be with the obvious stakeholders. Eoin McLennan-Murray as a prison governor talks of the importance of communication and partnership with prisoners. He comments,

'Whatever we do in terms of communication is not enough. It is very important to give prisoners advance warning if there is going to be "lock in" in an evening with "association" (i.e. the opportunity to have a walk in the quadrangle with other prisoners) not possible. If you do not give advance warning you can build up resentment. Consistency of communication is crucial.'

For Eoin the partnership with prisoners is just as important as the partnership with staff to ensure the prison runs efficiently and there is no build up of resentment.

Colonel Bob Stewart, a former Infantry Battalion Commander in Bosnia, talks of building partnership with his senior officers when taking potentially dangerous decisions. He says he was given no mission, scarce intelligence and leaden rules of engagement. Stewart in a talk to the London Business Forum (20th September 2006) comments that throughout his career as an officer he tried to involve his soldiers in decision-making as much as possible. For example when he decided the battalion should base itself near a particular city, the scene of some of the war's heaviest fighting, he consulted his 40 officers. His view was that achieving a shared perspective was especially important in situations that required a completely unconventional response.

Key steps in building partnership might include reflecting on:

- Who are the potential partners (taking a wide definition of partners)?
- What are the main fears and concerns of partners?
- What would be the minimum ingredients of success for partners?
- What might be the most useful signals in terms of building partnership?
- What more could be achieved through effective partnership rather than through individual action?

Ensure effective engagement

There is a golden thread running through effective engagement which includes respect, listening, open-mindedness, flexibility, mutual support, challenge and looking forward. This often takes a long time to build up, but can be destroyed far more easily than it can be created.

Stanton Marris describe themselves as an 'organisational energy consultancy'. They have an outstanding track record of influencing focused change in national organisations. They have been focusing attention recently on what constitutes meaningful engagement. Their key learning from work with a wide range of organisations has been:

- Start with the business case of engagement – what are you trying to engage people with? What will the benefits be?
- Define engagement in language that is *meaningful* in your particular organisational context and to your key audiences (avoid the off-the-shelf frameworks).
- Convince your colleagues that engagement is more than a one-step process – it is a planned series of linked actions and supporting activities – for which leaders need new skills and confidence to use them.

- Clarify who is *responsible* for making engagement work – CEO, top team, leaders, Communications and HR (all of them).
- Use internal stories of *successful engagement* that have lead to measurable benefits and outcomes to illustrate what you mean by engagement – and to draw out the lessons of what works and what doesn't.
- Use the power and influence of people who have been involved in those successes to convince others of the benefits of a more thoughtful and planned approach.
- Introduce regular 'leading' indicators of engagement so that you can use the data to prioritise the right activity that will deliver the results you want – before it is too late.

Effective engagement makes it much easier to see how a decision is going to be received and provides a good basis to then move into making a firm decision.

Engagement may be about talking to people but it can also be about talking it through with yourself. Jane Willis comments,

> '*I will do a practical walk around a decision in my head. That may not impact on the decision itself but it will certainly make me more comfortable with the outcome. It makes it much easier to understand how a decision is going to be received. There are very few win-win situations. Normally there will be winners and losers. How you balance these in the decision-making is important.*'

Effective engagement is not only who you talk and listen to. It is about how you use your own thinking processes to engage with an issue and see it from different perspectives.

At the heart of good engagement is effective conversation which is dynamic and purposeful. (This is considered further my book *Conversation Matters: how to engage effectively with one another* (2005: Continuum)

Effective engagement in conversation is about:

- building trust and engendering openness;
- providing stillness amidst conversation to give others an opportunity to reflect;
- using humour to see the funny side of situations; and
- making conversation a shared journey of discovery.

Discernment is an important part of engagement covering:

- clarity of purpose in entering a conversation;

- questions that open up issues rather than close them down;
- curiosity aiming to understand why a particular issue is important to somebody;
- experimentation so that we are not always predictable creatures of habit;
- taking risks in terms of sharing; and
- brevity in drawing out clear points and conclusions.

Quality conversations where engagement is operating well:

- are dynamic: you cannot predict the end of a conversation at the start;
- include a healthy level of debate while working through difficult issues;
- transcend boundaries and provide challenge so that conversations are not inward looking or comfortable;
- bring freshness and express things in different ways; and
- include a compelling modesty with a strong focus on listening.

Some practical reflections might be:

- how good is your engagement with different stakeholders?
- what works particularly well for you in terms of building engagement?
- how do you want to further stretch that engagement?
- what mental processes might you go through so you are engaging within yourself with different perspectives and understanding the consequences of your decisions?

Building agreement

Moving on from building understanding to building agreement includes a focus on persuasion that works, building consensus, seeking agreement, reflecting on timing and ensuring the right information is available.

Persuasion that works

Juliet Erickson in her book, *The Art of Persuasion* says,

> *'Good effective communication brings the results we want by giving us the ability to make ourselves clearly understood, to build strong relationships and connections with others and to successfully persuade others to support us.'*

Her approach is based on:

- **forget rules:** i.e. tailor what needs to be said to address each of the party's particular interests and level of understanding;
- **awareness and flexibility:** being alert to what is happening and responding appropriately;
- **build rapport:** finding the common interest;
- **be yourself:** cultivating the ability to feel natural and relaxed in any situation;
- **focus on individuals:** not treating an audience as an amorphous blob of people;
- **be definite:** have a purpose or strong intent;
- **actions speak loudest:** effective communication involves behaviour, appearances, gestures and unspoken empathy;
- **stay present:** being aware of the moments you are in and not being lost in the past or the future.

Suma Chakrabarti as Permanent Secretary at the UK Department for International Development tells of the consequences of a decision to transfer resources to Iraq. There was a decision covering the work of the department that 90% of resources went to the poorest countries and 10% to middle income countries. When resources were to be transferred to Iraq this decision rule provided an important frame of reference. There was a need for a solution that was evidence based, was decisive and clear upfront with a rapid turnaround time. This meant reductions in the aid programmes in Latin America with the requirement to renegotiate these programmes within the countries concerned.

Steps that Suma and his colleagues took included he and some of his senior colleagues going to South America. On the basis that clarity and communication was essential they talked extensively with individuals who would be affected by this change of policy. They stood in front of staff and said why they had made this decision: the aftermath was that there were no rumblings about the outcome. Although expenditure levels were being reduced in South America there was greater freedom about how the money would be spent: therefore the department's officials in South America had less money but greater discretion about how it was used.

At an early part of this process a decision was needed by the board. There was a strong feeling among board members of having been on shared journeys over a number of years together. They could not and did not want to fudge the issue. There were two key directors who needed to be brought onside. What particularly helped with one of them was an appeal to his love of the organisation and his interest in where it was going. Board members spent time talking the issues through with him, they appealed to his communication skills saying that they could not do without him. For Suma it was well worth setting aside a day of his time to be available to talk through the issues with this key director until the point when a satisfactory outcome had been reached and the director was willing to be committed to the revised policy.

This was an example of a decision where there was no scope for a discussion about whether reducing funding in Latin America was right or wrong: the conversations were about how the decision was implemented. This involved signalling the reason for the decision and being clear what the scope of the discussions were about. The decision to provide local managers with greater flexibility about how the money was allocated helped enormously in enabling the department's staff in Latin America to see the continuing important value of their role.

John Saunders, the chief executive of the Institute of Public Finance tells a revealing story from his time as chief executive of the Security Industry Authority. It took some time for John, with industry leaders, to persuade the Home Office of the need for regulatory arrangements to ensure effective standards within the industry. John's learning was:

- we should have focused on influencing government at the most senior levels and continued our links at that level;
- we should have invested more in building trust with those individuals based on knowledge and understanding;
- we should have been mindful of when people did not understand our perspective and worked hard to build understanding; to know you are right is not enough!
- we should have watched the tag of being labelled as 'troublesome' and turned round that perception as quickly as we could;
- we were right to stick to our aspiration of improved regulations but there was much to learn in how to influence and persuade key people in government.

The key learning for John was the importance of being open to learn and change your approach if you are failing to persuade key players.

The essential ingredients of persuasion are:

- What is the message that has to be communicated?
- Who are supporters of the message and how can their support be brought into play?
- Who are the sceptics and what might be the best means of influencing them?

- What are the unavoidable features of the changes and what is the flexibility at the margins?
- What approach to persuasion has worked best before with this group?

Build consensus

Building consensus prior to announcing a decision can be important in preparing the way effectively. Archie Hughes sees the role of the chief executive as a sounding-board. He reflects that one of the smoothest ways of reaching a decision is when a key individual comes to talk to him in advance about their proposed conclusions before finally settling the conclusions and circulating them to a wider circle of people.

When a political decision needs to be taken there is often a difference between your view of what is right and what will carry weight with people from their perspective as stakeholders or customers. If a decision is 'right', but there is no buy-in, it is likely to have a minimum impact. Effective persuasion involves carrying people with you, even if there has to be compromise along the way.

Finlay Scott, the chief executive of the General Medical Council, talks of the importance of 'yesable propositions' in building consensus. If you are given a proposition and invited to say yes you are more likely to get the answer yes: it is more difficult for the hearer to say no as they have to explain their reason. Therefore putting a 'yesable proposition' is more likely to get the outcome you want than an even-handed description of two options.

An essential part of reaching a consensus is clarity about the extent to which a decision needs to be a shared corporate decision. If a decision is hatched up between two individuals but the corporate centre or leadership of an organisation is not involved, such as a decision may be doomed to failure. In any organisation clarity about the extent to which the centre or leadership want to be involved is an important piece of information. Clarity about whether the key stakeholders can live with a decision is important for success. For example for major decisions, any UK government department the Secretary of State must have the agreement of Treasury ministers, and on the biggest of issues, the Prime Minister, before next steps can be defined and taken forward.

It is not always possible to reach a consensus. Sometimes the decision has to be imposed. My younger son, Colin talks of his experience captaining ultimate frisbee teams at university, club and junior international levels. Ultimate frisbee is a rapidly growing sport with 7 players from each team on the pitch at any one time. It is a cross between American football and netball demanding very fit players because of the speed with which the disk is thrown from player to player. The captain has to make decisions very quickly about what moves to make and who to have on the pitch at any one time. Colin comments

> *'You have to make very quick decisions. You will have talked extensively in training about the game and will have practised sequences. But in the heat of the game you have to decide. There is no opportunity to consult. You have to rely on the degree of trust that has been built up. You need players both to take forward your decision and to do it with complete commitment. If they are half-hearted the point will be lost. The essential characteristic of a successful ultimate frisbee team is complete trust between captain and players which will take many hours of training and time together to build up.'*

This illustration demonstrates the importance of the leader building trust over a period and being shown to be trustworthy. Colin spends time with players after a game talking through why he made certain decisions. He needs to demonstrate that he does listen and modify his approach in the light of reactions from others but he must be willing to make quick decisions throughout a game based on his own judgement. His success as a leader depends on credibility built up through continuous communication with his players, listening to them, explaining his decisions, and developing the team's approach.

Key questions on building consensus might be:

- How important is reaching consensus for a particular decision to work?
- What is getting in the way of reaching consensus?
- Is the degree of trust strong enough for me to impose a way forward?
- Do I spend enough time explaining when I have imposed an answer?

Seek agreement

An e-mail often seems the obvious way of telling somebody about a conclusion you have reached and inviting them to agree. In many cases this might be the most efficient way of doing it. But there is always the danger that you view the sending of a decision from your outbox to somebody else's inbox as a success in itself rather than finding the most appropriate way to influence somebody to accept the conclusion that you are inviting them to reach.

Bahrum was clear about the right action but couldn't face up to the complicated discussion he would need to have with a member of his team. He wrote an e-mail instructing that an action be taken. The result was a rather half-hearted process. In retrospect he realised that what was needed was an open, honest conversation about the next steps with the individual to reach a point where this person felt, at minimum, that they had been heard, even if the solution was not their preferred way forward.

Dorcas Batstone is head of Stakeholder Assurance at Elexon and takes a lead on decisions affecting how the market operates within the electricity industry. Her belief is that it is better to get decisions into the open than let them fester. She is not afraid of making difficult decisions but recognises the need for people to see there is a framework for decisions with individuals knowing that she will be fair. Her approach is:

- be sure about the facts and cross check them if necessary;
- don't spring things on people;
- give people the opportunity to redeem themselves if you are being critical.

She says that she can be tough sometimes in taking decisions and that people will take that judgement in the end because they recognise the framework within which she is operating. What is crucial is building up a relationship so that if you make a wrong decision you can say so and win respect for changing your mind.

Her approach when auditing an organisation is:

- line the steps up carefully, warning people in advance that the audit is going to take place;
- prepare thoroughly in advance giving forewarning about lines of enquiry;
- prepare people for potentially bad news;
- take forward the enquiry in a calm, considered and unemotive way;
- take time to gauge people's likely reactions;
- reflect on the difference between what is likely to be the corporate reaction as well as the personal reaction.

Dorcas stresses that if you are going to write a critical report it is important to prepare people to receive bad news, telling them face-to-face and ensuring that senior people know directly from you rather than on the grapevine. She also stresses the importance of being clear what is the outcome you want in any such conversation. If a conversation gets difficult she is very clear that it is no excuse to be rude to people. For her, rudeness is inconsistent with her values and is likely to be counterproductive. There will be difficult patches in a professional relationship when outcomes have not been delivered. For Dorcas this involves a firm conversation rather than an emotive one. Destroying trust through rudeness can mean it takes a long time to rebuild that ability to work effectively together.

Reflect on the timing

The successful team player in sport knows that success is all about timing. The rugby pass has to be executed at just the right moment to avoid the outstretched hands of the opponents. Politicians spend many hours reflecting on the best timing for a controversial announcement. Companies watch carefully when to announce good news or negative stories.

A key question is when to decide and announce difficult decisions. Sometimes you need to wait until the last piece of information is available or another critic is signed up. On other occasions there is a moment to announce when the tide is going your way. If that moment is lost the tide may have turned against you.

How do you decide on the best timing for a decision? It will be a matter of seeking the best possible professional advice, the views of those closest to the customer and the perspective of your boss or sponsor. But sometimes it is just taking a 'flyer' on timing as no timing is perfect. Following your instinct having sought the best possible advice has often got to be the way forward. Whatever the decision about the timing of a decision or announcement, in many cases there is the opportunity to review the decision on a future occasion.

Ensure adequate information is available

Having adequate information to both make and implement difficult decisions is fundamental. Forward thinking is a prerequisite to having the information available to make difficult decisions and then to demonstrate that they are soundly based.

Peter Connew with his experience of implementing information management systems comments,

> 'Carefully planned information management is crucial – faced with a situation where decisions have to be made quickly, it is crucial to have confidence that the information needed for making the right judgements is available and accurate. It is important that information systems cover financial and non-financial considerations and essential that early warning mechanisms are embedded. There is a danger in organisations where information is largely focused on financial aspects, that management are not provided with a good understanding of how the business is performing. If profits are declining this should

be highlighted as early as possible. Ideally information systems should collect data that will enable downturns in sales or increases in costs to be predicted. In addition to volumetric and other typical data captured by some of the better examples, businesses should report on the changing attitudes of their staff and what is happening outside the business that may impact on it in the short and longer term. Good information systems promote and support accurate forecasting and identification of risks. It is important to avoid taking just a crude look at the figures without considering trends and comparisons with other similar organisations.'

There is an important feedback loop between the availability of up-to-date information and the building of agreement about next steps. The securer the evidence of progress through sound information, the easier reaching agreement becomes.

Taking action

After building understanding and agreement the elements of taking action include: communicating the outcome, being clear on the rationale, watching the cultural interpretations, having a sound feedback loop and being aware of the pitfalls.

Communicate the outcome

Any decision is only as good as the way it is communicated and received. So often huge effort goes into reaching the point of decision with the actual announcement left to a junior press officer. Central to success is the way a decision is communicated.

Clarity of message is so important. In big organisations you need to use organisational semaphore. The message has to be clear and uncluttered. It is very important not to take things for granted and not to nuance messages.

Clarity and repetition are central to effective communication. KISS (keep it simple stupid) is as good a starting point as any. Boiling down the key message so that it is brief, clear and unambiguous must be the right starting point. One government minister I worked with always applied the test of what will a decision or approach mean to the person living on a housing estate in a Yorkshire city. A message had to be crystal clear and relevant to pass this test as this minister knew that his constituents would recognise humbug when they saw it.

A danger for all leaders is that once they have made a decision they some-how believe that it has been instantly communicated from their head and that all sensible people will immediately accept that the decision is right. The plan for communicating a decision is just as important as the steps taken in making a decision. Although different methodologies may be used to communicate the same decision to different groups of people, the cen-tral message needs to be consistent or different interpretations will become evident and divisive.

A clear message can never be repeated too often. Consistency is an es-sential ingredient in building trust. If trust becomes blurred, commitment becomes less strong. Repetition of a consistent message with the same de-gree of freshness and enthusiasm to many audiences has to be at the centre of delivering difficult decisions. A test of effective communication is, 'can I explain it clearly to myself and others'?

Watch the cultural interpretation

Watching the cultural interpretation is an important element when a de-cision is to be announced. Understanding how a message is likely to be received in different cultures is crucial in fine-tuning the approach to an announcement.

Gordon Wetherell is an experienced UK Ambassador. For him a key in-gredient of the success in implementing a difficult decision or conveying a difficult message is the timing of the announcement and how you commu-nicate it. Whether you convey a difficult message in written form or orally it needs to take account of the cultural context. For some people the initial conveying of a message orally increases the chance of acceptance signifi-cantly. For others it is only receiving the message on paper which will per-suade them that action is intended. He tells of one case where a message critical of the recipient was conveyed on paper and copied to a number of people. The reaction was far more adverse than if a sequence of conversa-tions had taken place because of the cultural context in which the decision was communicated.

Be clear on the rationale

Essential to communicate an outcome well is being clear on the ration-ale for the decision. Bill Brackenbridge, the chair of a health authority in Scotland, talks of the importance in any decision that is controversial of a rationale that is visible to all. He is clear that he owes it to the rest of the Health Service that decisions he reaches are clear and based on sound information. There is a strong concern for fairness and for propriety both within the Health Service and in his own values. Bill reflects that an over-riding driver can be the fear of making a wrong decision and being found out and criticised in the press. This is a plus in terms of forcing you to be very clear on the reasons for a decision but can sometimes be an inhibiter from taking the right decision if there is the risk of criticism.

Have a sound feedback loop

When I was press secretary to two Secretaries of State part of my role was to observe how the different audiences were reacting. I was picking up perceptions from commentators and journalists and feeding them back to the Secretary of State. A continuous feedback loop was essential so the Secretary of State was aware how his decisions were being perceived.

An essential part of my work as a coach is helping individuals understand how they and their decisions are perceived. I will often talk to a range of staff, stakeholders, customers and the boss who often tell me much more than they say direct to the individual about both positive and developmental aspects. Having an effective feedback loop may involve the use of an external coach, written 360° appraisal or asking key interlocutors directly about their views on an individual.

Key questions will be:

- Are you getting measured feedback from others about how I am communicating?
- How do you both celebrate positive feedback about communication skills and respond to negative and developmental feedback?
- What sort of feedback about communication do you want to see in the future?
- Whose views do you trust enough to ask them directly for their feedback on your communication with others?

Be aware of the pitfalls

Potential pitfalls include:

- short-termism;
- being entrapped by your own spin;
- being led by media reaction;
- losing your cool.

Short-termism

For many leaders, especially politicians, the media reaction on the following day is so important. A leader is rightly worried about their reputation and the value of their 'stock', but sometimes individuals need to be protected from themselves where there is an over-reliance on short-term plaudits. The answer can be to keep coming going back to focusing on the long-term goals recognising that in the short-term there will be ups and downs. An individual captivated by short-termism will soon fall by the wayside through exhaustion.

Being entrapped by your own spin

It is important to be utterly convinced and convincing in putting across a message. There ought to be a congruence between the reasons why a decision is made and the way we explain it. Sometimes when we want to put a particular gloss on our explanation for a particular audience, it can blur the real reason for making a decision. Regularly coming back to the fundamental reason for a decision enables us to keep our feet firmly rooted so that we avoid being captivated by the way we want to communicate a particular message.

Being led by media reaction

Where there is a trusted relationship with a journalist there can be an openness in talking around a subject in a thoughtful way. But at the end of the day the journalist is there to write a story not to support you in developing your thinking. It is easy to fall into the trap of being taken in by a journalist. When talking with a journalist, however informal a conversation, every phrase has to be assessed by whether you would be happy for it to appear in a newspaper article.

A positive media response to a major decision is desirable, but not at any cost. Sometimes the adverse reaction to a decision has to be faced and absorbed. Appeasing the media for an easier life can lead to the most shambolic of decisions and a loss of clarity of vision.

Losing your cool

However cross the media coverage makes you, showing your anger is a recipe for disaster. There is nothing a journalist likes more than an individual losing their cool: that is the moment when points are made and instantly regretted. Where there is criticism there needs to be a sense of detachment and a long game. Sometimes an inaccurate comment needs to be correctly quickly, but stirring the story might be just what the journalist wants you to do. Keeping that sense of coolness and a measured purposefulness is essential while recognising that media comment can do untold damage to reputations which may take some time to rebuild.

Next steps

At every stage in making a decision communication is vital. Part of any meeting considering a difficult issue should include a reflection on what the communication issues are. The definition of communication needs to be wide enough to build understanding and build agreement as well as to take forward the action of communication.

Key questions are:

- Am I listening effectively to all the sources of intelligence available to me?
- Am I building partnerships and alliances with the right mix of people, recognising that some of them are long-term where there are no immediate benefits?
- Can I develop my approaches in building partnership and consensus?
- Can I strengthen my ability to engage effectively with a wide range of different people?
- What am I learning from decisions I see being taken and how best to communicate outcomes?
- Can I further develop my sources of feedback?

Part 2

Taking forward making difficult decisions

This section of the book picks out certain key themes in taking forward difficult decisions. These are essential building blocks in developing the capabilities further in making difficult decisions well. It looks in particular at:

- Applying the learning from good decision makers.
- Embedding the ability to make difficult decisions.
- Enabling others to make difficult decisions.
- Key questions in making difficult decisions.

This section aims to be practical in helping you develop your capabilities in each of these areas drawing from the practical experience of individuals from a range of different circumstances. Questions that might be relevant as you work through this section may include:

- What can I learn from good decision makers?
- How can I use my own experience to best effect, to embed the ability to make difficult decisions?
- How can I enable people to have the courage, confidence and resources to make their choices effectively?
- How can I develop my capability to ask the most useful questions?
- How can I create the type of moments which will enable me to take decisions well?

Chapter 6

Applying the learning from good decision makers

Increasing our ability to make difficult decisions well is often about watching others and deciding what is the learning from someone else's experience. This might be observing a national figure and seeing how they respond to new information, criticism and changed expectations. It might mean observing the way a leader in your organisation makes decisions and deciding what you want to take forward from their experience. It might mean observing yourself even harder and deciding what of your experience you want to emulate on future occasions.

This chapter looks at a number of different examples and invites you to reflect on what the learning might be from these particular illustrations. It then encourages you to reflect on a demanding decision you are likely to be in and how you might take decisions in that context drawing on the experience of others.

A rugby referee

Roger King referees rugby union matches at club level. As a referee he establishes boundaries at the start. He talks with the players at the beginning of a match stressing the importance of what happens when there is a tackle. He puts a lot of effort into building a rapport with the players. As a referee the key question about decision-making is finding the right balance between empathy and letting the players play and managing their behaviour in a fairly confrontational situation so that they stay within the laws of the game.

So the good referee does lots of preventative refereeing (e.g. talking people back onside), giving one or two early penalties so they know who is boss, but also being ready to step in firmly if there is a 'flashpoint' like a high tackle or a punch. Both sides will be nagging away at you. You give a penalty try when someone has been unfairly impeded. As a referee there needs to be a clear sense of justifiable decision. Hard decisions sometimes just have to be made, if you do not get your approach to decisions right the game can get blacker at every turn. Roger comments

> *The freeze-frame in your mind is very important when you call somebody over. After an infringement you blow the whistle and walk away nine or ten paces and ask someone to come over to you. The ten paces are important for the referee to gather his thoughts and to be detached from the other players. You buy yourself time to run the tape again. Reading the game is important. The tempo of the game is crucial. There can come a time when things escalate. If it is the fourth time when someone has been impeded you have to take action. You need to keep on top of things.'*

Roger says it takes courage to send someone off who you know will be difficult. But at the end of the game there is often the feedback 'I am glad you were brave enough to do that.' Roger puts a strong emphasis on communication. When a player comes back from the 'sin bin' Roger always talks with him to ensure he is coming back into the game with the right attitude. Roger will keep forewarning players when there is a potential infringement problem so there are no surprises and they are aware that they are in danger of infringing the rules.

As a referee, Roger is fully engaged with the players. He is talking with them and aware of their behaviours and emotions. He is firm with them, consistent in his messages and will take time to walk ten paces away when a very hard message has to be given to an individual.

Some of the learning from this story for us might be:

- Are we engaging enough with the people affected by the decisions we make?
- Are we trying to create a culture of no surprises when hard decisions have to be taken?
- Have we a technique like Roger's which creates space by allowing us to walk ten paces away and rerun an incident in our minds?
- Have we the courage to produce the yellow card or even the red card when it is necessary?

A Chief Constable

Paul West is the Chief Constable of West Mercia Constabulary. He talks of the principles which are most important in his leadership of a police force. These are performance focus, embracing diversity, integrity and quality people.

Paul says that a Chief Constable is rarely in the position of taking operational decisions in a crisis. It will be an Assistant Chief Constable who is more likely to be 'hands on' in a visible crisis. The Chief Constable needs to be seen as a fair minded leader in tune with people at all levels in the organisation. The Chief Constable's decisions have huge implications for people and for the future well-being of the organisation. Paul talks of seeing all police officers when they are recruited and all staff when they are promoted. In the conversations with new promotees he always gives advice on decision-making. He says,

'Often you do not have all the information you would ideally wish to have in a fast moving situation. But you are there to make a decision. If you take into account all of the information you could reasonably be expected to have available to you and make a balanced and pragmatic decision I will support you in what you have done. This is not an encouragement to make hasty or rash decisions. But you must have confidence that your decision-making will be supported by others.'

Some of Paul's practical advice about decision-making is as follows:

- First impressions can be deceptive. You should take time to get to know your staff. Don't rush to make judgements on people. Listen to the views of other managers and supervisors but form your own opinions on the respective strengths and developmental needs of your staff.
- Keep practising decisions in certain circumstances and then good decision-making will become semi-automatic.
- Remember that minor decisions can have major implications for staff: for example changing the shirt colour and style for police officers may seem on face value to be a minor decision but in reality is very important in terms of staff morale and organisational image.
- Small decisions need a basis of proper analysis: groundwork has got to be done well.

Paul talks of the key responsibility of a leader in making long-term decisions. The police on the ground will be particularly concerned about day-to-day pressures. But a Chief Constable must be very clear about the long-term strategy he or she is trying to embed. The senior leadership will be making judgements on long-term investment which might take three or four years to come to fruition. The Chief Constable has to have the strategic clarity to be able to do that. Part of making long-term strategic decisions is based on an open and inclusive relationship with the members of the police authority. Their different perspective is invaluable. Being a good police leader is fundamentally about managing risk well. If you are totally risk averse you will make no progress.

Paul talks of sometimes having to 'push yourself over the edge'. People need to see that you are taking key decisions. He reflects that a factor in ensuring good decisions are made in a timely fashion is the potential embarrassment of not being seen to be making a decision! That is a lever he occasionally uses on himself to ensure he makes effective decisions.

Paul talks of people in less senior positions sometimes appearing to be frustrated if he doesn't make a decision instantly. He says at times it can feel as if he is being pressed to make a decision on a whim. He will insist that he needs time to decide and will make clear that he must be given the space to do so. His advice to others when making difficult decisions is:

- gather as much factual information as you can;
- think through the potentially adverse implications;
- work through the 'what if' questions;
- think about the human element – what are the implications for people of your decision;
- reflect on whether the decision is going to have an impact on improving service delivery by the police force;
- be clear about the costs and related savings;
- let your intuition count as you work through the decision-making process;
- look at a problem from a range of different perspectives;
- have trusted sources of advice available to you;
- articulate what is leading you to a particular conclusion in order to help clarify the arguments.

Paul is clear that one of the roles of a senior police officer is to aim to reduce the fear in others about their decisions going wrong. He routinely says to newly promoted supervisors,

> *'You are a substantive sergeant and are expected to make decisions. I understand how you feel. I have been in your position. I recognise that there is a fear about things going wrong if you make the wrong call.'*

One of the key learning points from this illustration is Paul's clarity that it is his job to make decisions at the strategic level and it is the task of other people in a police force to make hands-on decisions in particular operational situations while he retains overall accountability for the quality of decisions across the police force. It is very clear that the tone the Chief Constable sets is vital for the effectiveness and morale of a police force.

The lessons from this illustration are readily transferable. Key questions that might arise for you are:

- Am I clear about the level at which I need to make decisions?
- How am I building up the confidence of people in my organisation to make decisions effectively?
- Am I setting the right balance between the collection of factual information and the need to be decisive?

- Am I spending enough time setting the right tone for decision-making within my organisation?
- Am I building up people's confidence enough within the organisation that that they are able to have confidence in their own decision-making?
- Am I insisting on being given space when pressed to make instant decisions?

A High Court Judge

Sir Jeremy Cooke is a High Court Judge in the Commercial Court and is now a Presiding Judge with responsibility for the oversight of many members of the judiciary in the South East of England. He talks of absorbing the facts, writing down the key points for and against and then reaching a judgement between well populated arguments when sitting in the Commercial Court. The starting point is to be very clear on what he needs to decide and focusing on that. He sees ascertainment of the right questions as absolutely vital to making the right decision. That applies both to judicial decisions and management decisions.

In the judicial context, he talks of watching the emotional elements and looking at the emotional reactions of individuals in the witness box.

> 'You watch to see how the emotional ramifications play out. You grapple with vested interests. You draw on your experience of life. You draw on your own wisdom about how you would react and how you have seen others react in particular situations. You watch the body language and demeanour of witnesses'.

In the context of adjudication in commercial cases, he talks of weighing up the facts and watching to see when inconsistencies emerge between the evidence given, the contemporaneous documents and the commercial probabilities taking account of people's reactions when a problem surfaces. He suggest that the immediate reaction of the parties is important and often reveals the true situation before there is time to develop, with the aid of lawyers, well formulated, self-justifying arguments.

In the judicial context his advice on decision-making from his experience as a senior judge involves the following:

- Ensure that you have good and full information. Be clear what the key facts are.
- Sift what is relevant and what is irrelevant.
- Be clear what it is you have to decide.

- Use your experience of life and understanding of people to determine the truth.
- Make a clear analysis of the arguments for and against.
- Express the decision with clarity.

Sir Jeremy Cooke's perspective is that all these points hold good for management decision-making, with the following additions.

- Understand what the organisation is expecting of you.
- Be aware of the context and environment in which you are operating.
- Know whom to consult and from whom support is available, both amongst peers and those accountable to you and to whom you are accountable.
- Be confident in the decisions made.
- Build your personal resilience.

The key learning from the experienced senior judge is about the balance between thorough analysis and acute observation.

Practical questions for us from this illustration might be:

- Are we clear that we have got the key questions adequately defined?
- Can we become an even more acute observer?
- Are we watching people's emotions enough in order to assess consistency and commitment?
- Are we seeking out the advice of peers in a way which helps us reach difficult decisions where there may be ambiguity?

A UK Ambassador

Gordon Wetherell was until recently the UK Ambassador in an African country. Gordon talks of making decisions in difficult situations where people may need to be airlifted out of areas of conflict. Gordon talks about making sure you have all the facts about people's whereabouts and the conditions they are in. You need to be very clear what you are going to ask the host government for. He sees as particularly important the differential roles of different people in the operation. There needs to be clarity about what are the expectations on individuals within the embassy. The communications people are vital. The operation needs to be managed thoroughly as a project.

Gordon sees as the ambassador's main roles in a situation where people are in danger as, leadership of their team and clarity about who does what, and contact at the most senior levels of the host government to ensure that the appropriate cooperation and authority (e.g. to bring in aeroplanes to evacuate people) are obtained. The ambassador's effort put into building long-term relationships of trust with senior leaders in the host country can pay rich dividends in these circumstances. In short, the ambassador should concentrate on what only the Head of Mission can do or where they can add most value. Another key element of the ambassador's role is visibility, including the ability to handle questions from the press well. When people have to be evacuated Gordon talks of putting his deputy in charge of running the project from the mission while he would need to be visible at the reception point talking to evacuees, senior politicians and to the media. Gordon's advice is,

> 'You get as clear a picture of the facts as you can. You make quick decisions on allocating responsibilities. You get the communication focus right. As a leader you do what only you can. You need to keep cool. You need to reassure people. The basic principles are about getting the facts at the beginning, getting the line to communication right and being clear of where you can add value.'

The lessons from the experience of a senior ambassador are about the importance of building strong relationships, making quick decisions on allocating responsibilities, getting the communication focus right and being clear on how different people can contribute most effectively.

Some of the practical questions for us from this illustration might be:

- Are we building the right long-term relationships which will stand us in good stead if there is a crisis?
- Are we clear how we would make quick decisions on responsibilities in a crisis?
- Have we got the communication focus right and would our communication arrangements work where urgent decisions need to be taken?
- Are we clear about the value-added role of different key people in a crisis?

A chief executive

Lesley Strathie is the chief executive of Jobcentre Plus which is a national UK organisation employing 65,000 people involved in encouraging people back into employment and paying benefits to individuals. Lesley talks of the importance of asking for the right data. She is naturally evidence based.

For Lesley, learning by doing is how she has built up her capability to make decisions. She talks about the importance of learning through trial and error.

For Lesley, key elements of leadership are finding the key that unlocks people and finding the best people. A leader is somebody who has strong operational knowledge and good emotional intelligence. It is about understanding how best to make organisations work effectively but also how to motivate individuals to give of their best.

When it comes to making difficult decisions, Lesley talks of being pragmatic. Her instinctive reaction, developed over long experience, is important. But she always listens carefully to advice as it is important that there is a clear audit trial for decisions.

When asked to make decisions quickly she talks of giving the best answers she can in the time available. If it has to be instant, it will be instant. But she will not let people press her into making a decision before it needs to be made. For Lesley, learning by doing is how she has built up her capability to make decisions. There is the balance between being willing to make a quick decision, if that is what the situation requires, while not being willing to be pushed into a decision earlier than necessary.

Relevant questions from this example might be:

- How willing are we to learn by experience recognising that trial and error is important?
- How good are we at differentiating between situations where we need to make a quick decision and a context where we can create ourselves a little bit of time?
- How good are we are ensuring there is an audit trial for our decisions which is properly recorded?
- How best can we unlock the potential in people so that they are fully motivated?

Observing others effectively

In this chapter we have looked at a number of people who make decisions in high profile situations. We have drawn some practical lessons from their approach and identified some key questions that might be relevant for us.

A very practical way of developing our ability to make difficult decisions is to observe others, note down what they do well and see what questions that raises for us in making decisions. This observation can be of a national figure or a leader in your area of work, community or family. Often the best learning comes from observing someone making quick practical decisions. Observing the teacher making decisions to motivate their pupils or a police officer managing the traffic after an accident or a speaker handling a situation where all the technology goes wrong can provide practical pointers in terms of clarity and keeping calm.

A key set of questions when observing others making decisions might be:

Clarity

- Did they show that they had been willing to analyse the situation thoughtfully?
- How did they use the information available to them effectively?
- Are you clear what success would look like?

Conviction

- How did their values or principles shine through?
- Did they use past experience to good effect or did it blinker their approach?
- Is there the capability and will to take forward a decision effectively?
- Is your experience telling you that success is likely and how can you increase the likelihood of success?

Courage

- How well did they cope with critics or setbacks?
- How well did they keep their cool in trying circumstances?
- How can you ensure you stay focused?

Communication

- Were they listening to and engaging with those who had an interest?
- How effectively did they persuade their stakeholders and customers?
- Is there consistency of message at each stage?

A next step might be to turn your observation on others into next steps for you in terms of taking forward your capacity to handle difficult decisions well in the future.

Handling a forthcoming demanding decision

How will you tackle a forthcoming demanding decision drawing on the experience of good decision makers? Can you reflect on a difficult decision you have to take?

Clarity

- Are you adequately clear about the issue, the problem and the context?
- Is there enough analysis available with proper account taken of risks?
- Are there ways forward with objectives and options and thought through consequences?

Conviction

- What is your intuitive judgement, values, past experience, trained judgement and emotional awareness telling you?
- Can you test your developing convictions through standing back, keeping calm and talking it through with a colleague, a mentor and your coach?

Courage

- How easy is it to turn belief into action and have the courage to act?
- Have you had the opportunity to reflect on where compassion or coherence fit in?
- Are there ways you can best ensure progress through overcoming fears, building in feedback and resilience and learning from mistakes?

Communication

- Can you build greater understanding through listening, building partnerships and ensuring effective engagement?
- Are there further steps in building agreement through persuasion that works or building consensus?
- What focus might there be on further action which involves communicating the outcomes, clarity of rationale, watching the cultural interpretation and having a sound feedback loop?

Next steps

As you consider forthcoming decisions it can be helpful to reflect on where you are now on a score of 1 to 10 on each of the 4Cs and what it would take to move a couple of notches higher. For example if the score of 1 is low and 10 high you might score yourself in relation to a particular decision as:

- 5 on clarity about alternative ways forward
- 3 on your current strength of conviction about the right way forward
- 4 about your courage level in making the decision, and
- 5 on the quality of communication so far about the issue

You might reflect on

- What further analysis would be needed for the clarity score to move from 5 to 7?
- What would need to happen for your level of conviction about the right outcome to move from 3 to 6?
- Who might you talk the issues through with so that your courage level moves from 4 to 6?
- What further steps might be put in place so that your confidence in the quality of communication rises from 5 to 7?

A simple numerical approach as above can help as a tool when deciding where to focus thought and action.

Chapter 7

Embedding the ability to make difficult decisions

The theory about difficult decisions may seem fine. We understand the interrelationship between clarity, conviction, courage and communication and we know how to analyse a problem, but what next? How do we embed the ability to take difficult decisions well and then do that consistently in a demanding and exposed role?

What are we embedding?

We all have some natural strengths when taking difficult decisions: it is applying those skills successfully and consistently which is the stretch. We all find some aspects of decision-making more difficult. Addressing those aspects can include:

- observing others and seeing what works for them;
- experimenting with different approaches and seeing what works for us;
- getting feedback from others about what types of approaches to decision-making have worked well and what less well; and
- being explicit to ourselves about how we are developing our approach to decision-making in different types of circumstances.

A perspective from the assistant principal of a sixth form college

Godalming College is a highly successful sixth form college with over 1500 students: it has won a sequence of awards and been recognised as a Beacon College by the UK National Learning and Skills Council. May O'Keefe, the assistant principal responsible for curriculum and quality, describes a number of strands which have been important to her in embedding the ability to take difficult decisions including:

- not always believing your way is the right way;
- recognising the impact difficult decisions will have on others;
- drawing on your previous experience effectively;
- recognising the importance of valuing the individual whatever the decision is;
- being open and friendly and at the same time circumspect and holding yourself back; and
- building respect from others in the consistency of your decisions.

May talks of a balance between being clear in your own mind and not always believing your way is the right way. She talks of strategic decisions where there is sometimes a diversity of view. She comments,

'I will put my case clearly but I won't pursue it if it will damage the unity of the team. It is important to see a decision from both the individual point of view and from the organisational perspective. You need everyone on board to take forward a difficult issue. Very few things are black and white. It is important to see things from each individual leader's point of view and then reach a compromise taking the agreed way forward in a positive way.'

For May, effective teamworking in taking difficult decisions involves the team being honest and open with each other, listening to each other, testing out ideas and then being willing to come to a shared and agreed way forward.

May comments that the most difficult decisions are often day-to-day ones. It is a matter of judging the effect a decision will have on the behaviour of the individual in the future. May is particularly skilled at motivating senior staff. She describes her thought process as,

'If I take a particular step will it maximise the individual's self-esteem and their value? It is very important to enable a member of staff to be feel good about themselves even when you are giving a hard message. It is getting the balance right in terms of getting the best out of each individual. If there are difficult messages I will always start with a positive and then talk about areas for development. The key question is, how do I motivate the individual to feel good about their next steps?'

'This is a skill I have had to develop. I have had to learn how to read an individual and give time to thinking about how I would feel in their shoes. The key thing as a leader is getting to know your people well and understanding the learning processes each individual goes through. My role is always to be constructive and able to grow each individual effectively.'

May recognises that she draws on her previous experience as a teacher in her role as assistant principal: she regards none of her previous experience as having been wasted. The skills in engaging and motivating staff are very similar to the skills needed to motivate and engage students.

A key theme of May's experience is recognising the importance of valuing the individual whatever the decision. She reflects,

'People will go with difficult decisions if they feel valued. If the leader takes decisions on the basis of clear shared values they are more likely to be accepted. If you are taking something away from an individual you have to be clear why. Why is the decision being made? How does it

fit in with the values of the organisation and the way the individual is valued? At the heart of this is always trying to put yourself in someone else's place to understand how they are likely to react.'

May sets out a very interesting balance between being open and friendly on the one hand and being circumspect and holding yourself back on the other. She comments about the dangers of letting your emotional reactions get in the way. She comments,

'When I have taken bad decisions, it has been when I have been pushed by emotional reactions. I have learnt through my mistakes when emotional reactions have clouded my judgement. I have learnt to be very circumspect, very measured and very calm. Sometimes you have to hold yourself back. You are affecting people's income and status.'

A key aspect of individuals being ready to accept decisions is the respect in which the decision maker is held. May comments,

'The way you take little decisions is crucial to the well-being of an organisation. They set a tone of trust. They set the context for big decisions. You have to build the respect from people through little decisions in order for big decisions to be accepted on the basis of shared trust.'

May sees this respect taking quite a long time to build up with the possibility that it can be lost very quickly. If the leadership is too top-down, respect can quickly go and the result is non-compliance.

The practical and thoughtful views of May O'Keefe as an assistant principal of a sixth form college demonstrate that often the most skilled people in making difficult decisions are not the strategic decision makers at national level. The most effective decision makers are often those at the interface between strategic decision-making and operational effectiveness. May is both a member of the college board dealing with strategic issues but also has significant operational leadership responsibilities ensuring the college is run effectively.

One way of learning how to embed the ability to make difficult decisions is to talk to individuals with operational responsibility to take forward strategic decisions in order to learn from their experience. For example:

- a deputy head in a school;
- a senior administrator in a hospital;
- a deputy prison governor;
- a regional director in a finance institution;

- the manager of a large supermarket;
- a plant manager in a manufacturing organisation.

Recognising that embedding the ability to make difficult decisions is not linear

Embedding the ability to take difficult decisions is not a linear process. As we learn from experience we become increasingly effective at taking difficult decisions but there will always be moments of self-doubt. Part of the way of coping with moments of self-doubt is the recognition that these moments do happen and are unavoidable. There is a difficult judgement about the extent to which these moments are revealed to others and the extent to which they are part of an inner dialogue. The answer will differ for different individuals but may well include:

- when there are severe moments of self-doubt in making a difficult decision;
- taking some quiet moments to look at the decision from a range of different perspectives;
- doing something completely different which you do well that will raise your confidence and enable you to come back to the difficult decision with new energy;
- sharing your doubts and reservations with one or two trusted advisers and listening to their questions and perspective;
- imagining you have taken the first step on a difficult decision and seeing how painful that feels;
- recognising that you have been on this journey before with a pattern of three steps forward and two steps back;
- accepting that on another day your mood will have changed and sometimes it is a matter of gritting your teeth for a while and not expecting an easy answer.

Creating structures which help embed the ability to make difficult decisions

Sometimes it isn't a matter of self-doubt but more a matter of self-discipline. Charles is a Crown Prosecutor who makes decisions deciding whether people will be brought to prosecution or not. He has to take reasoned risks. He comments,

'I can ask for more and more information but I must take a view on the basis of my legal knowledge and experience. This must come from within. Sometimes too many "what if" questions can be a major cause of delay. The key thing is to concentrate hard on what is relevant. A key part of the solution is to manage a case in your own mind and set clear timescales.'

For Charles, having a positive frame of mind was important when he came to make a difficult decision. We talked about sometimes giving himself an hour to focus on all the considerations as a means of concentrating his mind on all the aspects and then making a decision. It is about creating a pattern of decision-making which helps him reach an outcome. Charles talks about key factors of disciplining his thought processes and removing distractions. His imagination is important in terms of reflecting on what he could prove with the facts. He then needs to be assertive in the way he asks questions to get relevant information and then be focused on what the key facts demonstrate. He needs to be as clear as he can be in his own mind with the information available to him, and then face the risk that sometimes you do not always get it right.

For Charles as a Crown Prosecutor, embedding the ability to make difficult decisions is a combination of:

- being increasingly disciplined in the way he weighs up facts;
- being clear when he is convinced about a particular judgement: i.e. he is willing to stand up before a judge and be confident that he is right;
- having the courage to make a judgement on the basis of his past experience and his weighing up of the facts, and then to have the courage to argue the case convincingly; and finally
- reflecting on how he is going to communicate his views persuasively to the judge.

Techniques to embed the ability to make difficult decisions

Different individuals advocate different techniques for embedding the ability to make difficult decisions. Frank regularly used an approach of:

- grip yourself;
- grip your teeth; and
- grip your task.

When Frank faced a difficult decision he felt uneasy, became unsettled and lacked confidence in his own judgement. He needed to talk to himself in these situations to grip himself and his emotions. He then felt he needed to grip himself a second time in order to take the actual decision. For Frank it meant physically putting his teeth together and with clenched teeth taking a firm decision. His next step was about being clear how he was going to grip the task itself. Frank talked of courage linked to confidence and inner strength. Decision-making did not come easily to him but this sequence of three steps of gripping to make progress proved to be an effective technique for him.

As he used this approach of three grips on a repeated basis he embedded the ability gradually to take difficult decisions. Over time the teeth clench became less severe and was more like a minor ritual before taking a decision.

The importance of focus

Embedding the ability to make difficult decisions often depends on the ability to focus well. This can be increasingly difficult in a world where the challenges leaders face are more numerous, varied and complex than ever before.

In his paper called, 'Executive focus: how leaders lose it and how to regain it' (2004, *Development Dimensions International*) Matthew J. Paese emphasises the deleterious effect of an insufficient opportunity to focus, which can cause significant lapses in judgement and performance.

His thesis is that it is not uncommon for leaders to lose focus because:

- work and information volume is staggering;
- job demands stretch leaders beyond their capabilities;
- job demands change quickly and often; and
- focus is pulled onto many different topics for very short periods of time, day after day.

Matthew suggests that when decision-making windows are brief, information volume is enormous, with judgements needing to be made quickly, the opportunity to sit, ponder and reflect is difficult to obtain. He suggests that leaders are often in a focus change mode and rarely in focus depth mode. As the leader learns to fly from topic to topic they become adept at short-term problems but do not have that opportunity to go into much depth focusing on key issues.

Matthew suggests that if a leader spends a brief moment thinking about an employee whose performance has suddenly slipped, one set of judgements will apply. But if the same leader spends 20 minutes thinking quietly about the same topic, making a few notes about the issues, different judgements may well emerge. These later judgements are much more likely to reflect a well-prepared, appropriate response than the former initial reaction.

Embedding the ability to focus is more than planning. For Matthew it is about taking the time and using the right process to understand important matters in depth. It is about occasionally taking the time and energy to examine carefully the nuances of the environment, so that clarity and consistency can be retained during times of pressure and ambiguity. He argues that three areas must be brought into focus and aligned namely:

- **Business focus:** a common understanding of what the organisation is trying to achieve.
- **Role focus:** clarity about the individual's contribution to the overall enterprise.
- **Self-focus:** accuracy and honesty in assessing the individual's ability to deal with the challenges.

Success in a faster faster world

Heather Dawson, a colleague at Praesta Partners, in her paper on 'Thriving in a Faster Faster World' talks of thriving in a world where there is far less time for leaders to settle into bigger and more demanding roles, these roles hold challenges that are numerous and complex, with decision-making becoming faster with little room for re-consultation and reflection.

Heather draws both from her experience and that of her colleague coaches at Praetsa Partners in suggesting that the key skills and disciplines are:

- shaping the role of work in one's life;
- managing communication technologies;
- finding the time to think and focus;
- leading amidst uncertainty and ambiguity;
- creating one's own oxygen tent; and
- understanding one's trigger point.

These interrelated themes of deep focus, striking the right balance of work in one's life, nurturing your sources of energy and knowing the boundaries of your emotional resolve have resonated with many of our clients as they face difficult decisions.

Next steps

The next steps in embedding the ability to take difficult decisions depends on your current starting point. An approach might be to self-assess (on a scale of 1 to 10 with 10 as very good and 1 not very developed) how good are you at taking decisions about:

- long-term strategic issues;
- short-term decisions about the use of your own time;
- decisions which mean persuading others to do things;
- decisions where it can be painful because of the emotional response from others; and
- decisions which have financial consequences.

Having scored each element then ask yourself what would have to happen for you to move one point up the scale: for example from point 2 to point 3. If there are three key steps that need to be taken to increase that ability to make decisions what can you do to enable those steps to happen?

Embedding the ability to make difficult decisions is not straightforward. It takes time to make progress. It is sometimes three steps forward and two steps back. Constant vigilance is needed to avoid becoming complacent or too fixed in our ways. It is often only when you look back that you see the progress that has been made.

Chapter 8

Enabling others to make difficult decisions

Successful leadership is not only what the leader does. It is also what the leader enables others to do so that they become increasingly effective in the contributions they make. Perhaps the biggest step change in leadership is when an individual moves from judging themselves by the effectiveness of what they achieve, to judging themselves by what others deliver under their overall guidance; hence the importance of developing the ability to enable others to take difficult decisions.

An illustrative case study: the assistant principal of a sixth form college

In the previous chapter we looked at the experience of May O'Keefe, the assistant principal of Godalming Sixth Form College, in embedding within herself the ability to make difficult decisions. Her success as a senior member of staff in a sixth form college is dependent on her ability to enable others to make difficult decisions. The principles underlying her approach are enabling others to:

- explore an issue from different angles in a professional environment;
- feel in control of the decision;
- remove the fear of failure; and
- demonstrate her strong support for the person making the decision.

When May is working with senior staff she is constantly trying to help them be more confident in making difficult decisions. Her approach is often to encourage an individual to look at a decision from different angles. She gives them space to reflect from different perspectives. She brings an understanding of the wider context and the ability to express thoughts or suggestions without being dogmatic which enables her to mentor people without them feeling threatened. Her belief is that the more an individual looks at a problem from different angles the increasingly effective they become at seeing the wider implications and the best way forward.

May talks about creating a professional environment in her office. By having the room tidy and ordered she wants to give the aura that she is a professional person talking with somebody who is also professional and therefore able to make a decision effectively. Her belief is that by being confident herself and demonstrating that she is in control of her own time and energy some of that sense of self-control will be encouraged in the person she is talking with. Her belief is that if she feels confident and calm, others will have confidence in her, and they themselves will become more in control of their own next steps. Crucial in this process is that sense of engagement between her and the individuals she is talking with. For May being a good manager depends on having all her ducks in a row, and being open to listen.

Her aim is to embed in the individuals she is talking with the ability to keep calm and to create mind space to think through an issue. Her aspiration is to take such discussions at a pace that will enable an individual to be totally objective and think things through carefully.

Her biggest ally in making difficult decisions herself is her husband because of the objectivity he brings. May will often say to her husband in the morning that she has a difficult decision she would like to talk through with him that evening. May aims to embed this reflective approach in her senior staff encouraging them to take time out to think an issue through carefully using a trusted other as a sounding board.

Part of her advice to others is

- you need a mechanism to stop and think;
- take time out to try out ideas;
- never make a decision on the hoof if you can possibly avoid it; and
- you have to learn some things by making mistakes: you have to learn by doing.

For May one of the secrets of enabling individuals to take difficult decisions is to take the fear out of decision-making. She says that once an individual is gripped by fear, logic will disappear. People do not tell the truth when they are frightened. May emphasises that if you are enabling an individual to face up to a difficult decision you need to take away the fear of blame so the individual makes the decision on the basis of what they think is right and not whether they will be blamed if it goes wrong. Good decision-making must involve taking away the likelihood of blame. Her perspective is, 'How can I support you once you have made a decision'.

May is very clear that senior managers are watched very closely by their staff. If the senior manager wants to embed effective decision-making in their staff they need to be consistent, building trust and shared values. For May the good decision maker will be embedding that ability to make decisions in their staff through lots of dialogue, rarely making top-down decisions without sounding out the views of individuals. People will go along with decisions that have been made in haste where they accept the necessity of speed, because they respect the person who is taking the decision and trust the way they have taken decisions in the past.

For May, one of the most important things a leader can do is set the tone to enable individuals to take difficult decisions after careful reflection and without fear. It can take a long time to build up the atmosphere of trust and support for decision-making. But, however well the atmosphere has been built up, it will be fragile and can be dissipated very quickly.

Effective engagement at the heart of good decision-making

Effective engagement is at the heart of any relationship that is working well. It must be at the centre of any mentoring of individuals to enable them to make difficult decisions well. The leader who is aiming to embed this ability in their colleagues may well be applying the same principles about the relationship between coach and client which Robin Linnecar and I set out in our book, *Business Coaching: Achieving Practical Results Through Effective Engagement.* We talk of the 'golden thread' running through effective engagement including the following characteristics:

- **respectful**, including trust and unconditional mutual regard;
- **listening**, being fully present and giving someone sole, undivided attention;
- **open-minded**, banishing pre-conceived notions, being fully on the individual's agenda and finding the point of need;
- **flexible**, varying the approach, place and timing to fit the circumstances of the individual;
- **supportive**, bringing encouragement, emphasising the positive and helping individuals to keep up their energy; and
- **challenging**, an engagement between equals working through a common problem.

Where an individual leader is embedding the ability to take difficult decisions in their colleagues the engagement between the two of them needs to be on a variety of different levels. It should be:

- **factual:** being on the same page in terms of information;
- **intellectual:** which involves talking about issues on equal terms in a robust way seeing the policy and operational consequences of different decisions;
- **emotional openness:** with an openness about human strengths and frailties creating a relationship where the colleague is willing to be open about their emotional reactions, recognising what they find difficult and how they want to develop their own capacity for courage and resilience; and
- **transformational:** which is about not having a fixed perspective on someone's ability to make difficult decisions but a belief that their capacity can improve and develop. It involves a shared creativity enabling a colleague to grow in their capacity to take difficult decisions well.

The importance of standing back

Suma Chakrabarti as a permanent secretary in the UK civil service talks of the importance of working through others. He sees his role as a senior leader being increasingly as an adviser to enable others to make difficult decisions rather than always making them himself. Part of his approach is to enable an individual to build their own successes in decision-making and then ensure that the individual knows that he will support them when they make subsequent decisions. He sees embedding the ability in individuals to make difficult decisions as significantly helped by:

- hanging on to the successes that an individual had in the past in making difficult decisions;
- deciding how to push the boundaries in terms of previous rules that have applied on previous occasions; and
- using a range of conversations, with both interested and impartial individuals to help bring clarity into the decision-making.

Sometimes the best way to enable someone to take a difficult decision is not to engage with them on that subject at all. Many parents have learnt by hard experience that when a son or daughter has a difficult decision to make the most appropriate help may be to provide time and space for relaxation with pampering and humour. The more a parent stands back and provides practical support and uncritical love, the easier it is for a son or daughter to make a difficult decision based on their own criteria and not based on the expectations of parents.

The same approach can work well with mentees or your own staff. Recognising an individual's generic qualities and skills will enable them the to make difficult decisions more easily and embed the ability to do so in the future.

Following your instinct

Jane Frost has held senior roles in both the private and public sectors, making decisions ranging from which programme to commission at the BBC and what type of campaigns to commission to ensuring tax payers pay their taxes. Her advice to someone embedding the ability to make difficult decisions is:

- immerse yourself in the environment of the people you are trying to influence;
- be willing to put time into key relationships;
- read the research but recognise that experts often put issues in a way that assumes people are always logical;
- think through carefully why people behave as they do in particular circumstances;
- don't shy away from hard decisions; and
- be willing to trust your instinct, recognising that this is often a 'short cut computer programme' after you have internalised the factual and psychological evidence you have received.

Building trust in others

At the heart of the skill to make difficult decisions is enabling someone to build trust relationships effectively with others. In their excellent book entitled *Trust Matters: for organisational and personal success*, authors Bibb and Koudi suggest that trusted leaders:

- have insight into themselves;
- create an atmosphere and expectation of trust, take responsibility;
- have clear intent and are honest without hidden agendas;
- have the organisation's and employee's best interests at heart;
- have credibility, are consistent, trust others;
- let others see their passion and it is obvious what they care about;
- speak from the heart not just from their intellect;
- confront people without being confrontational;
- do not mind admitting they do not know; and
- use power positively.

Building the ability to make hard decisions is about enabling others to build trust relationships effectively so that hard decisions can be made within a clear framework. When there is trust it is easier to look through unintended consequences, risks and uncertainties, without destroying the relationship.

Next steps

Enabling others to make difficult decisions is an invaluable contribution we can make to their development. It might be worth reflecting on:

- How did other people help embed in you the ability to make difficult decisions?
- Have other people given you feedback about how you have helped them take difficult decisions?
- Who have you seen struggle with difficult decisions: what has worked best in enabling them to take difficult decisions well?
- Who could you help make difficult decisions more easily?

Chapter 9

Key questions when making difficult decisions

What is the most important attribute when making difficult decisions? Is there one thing which matters more than anything else? There could be a range of different answers including: clear strategic thinking, a strong sense of vision, seeing the long-term consequences clearly, being focused on the right priorities, or having very good antennae about the attitudes and motivation of different people.

Perhaps the most important skill is the ability to ask the right question in the right way. The most significant contribution that a leader can make at a time when difficult decisions have to be taken is thinking through what the key questions are and how to ensure effective answers. This isn't about a deluge of a hundred and one questions. It is the questions that go to the heart of the matter that bring clarity to the consideration of next steps. It is partly a matter for the leader to be able to ask the key questions: but it is also the ability to encourage this skill within the group of people involved in a decision or using an outside independent person effectively to provide a source of impartial thoughtful questioning.

The right questions

The best of questions will rarely come completely intuitively. Even a few moments thought can lead to a question that hits the nail on the head. The briefly scribbled two questions on the pile of papers for a meeting on a difficult subject can be a means of crystallising where you think the focus of discussion and conclusion should be. How do you get to the right question? It might be talking through the issues with others, meditating round a topic or getting into the right frame of mind by going for a walk.

So what is the right question? Sometimes it will be a closed question to try to reach a firm conclusion. On other occasions it will be an open question to draw out some of the elements that need to be clarified before a decision can be taken. The best of leaders will signal when and why they are asking closed questions or open questions. Their whole demeanour and body language will reinforce whether the conversation is about focused precise answers or about exposing an issue and taking the thinking to another stage.

What matters is not just the nature of the question, it is the type of relationship between those in the conversation. If an individual feels completely on the defensive even the best of questions will just be parried away. The first step in asking the right question must be to create a relationship where an individual is willing to listen and be open to new possibilities. Building the trust for a question to work may take many years, but it can equally well be built up in a couple of minutes if urgent decisions have to be taken and there is evidence that the individuals are 'on the same page' with a common difficult issue to tackle.

Sometimes the best questions flow one from another. Once a relationship has been established there can be a killer question which goes to the heart of an issue and enables a crystallisation of next steps. For any leader it is both expressing clearly and then listening carefully in response. Do we create an atmosphere in which hard questions can be asked? Do people feel they always have to modify the way they put questions so as not to go against the party line or offend? When a question is asked do you hear the intent behind the question? You may not want to hear the intent, but is there a willingness to sit inside the shoes of the person asking the question so that you appreciate its full significance?

Key reflections are:

- When you ask a question how do you frame it so that you get the quality of response you need?
- How do you ensure that your question is not cluttered with your own preconceptions?
- How do you keep out the noise that is buzzing in your mind so that the way you ask the question and the way you hear the response is unambiguous?

As you move into discussions about difficult subjects with a boss the key questions might be: what are your expectations; what is success; what is the value-added you want from me? The unasked question most frequently in your mind might be: in what way is your success linked to what I am able to do? To your own staff the best of questions might be eliciting information about their strengths, motivations, hopes and aspirations. It will be enabling them to identify the risks clearly and unambiguously. Good questions will be building the sense of both challenge and mutual support. The conclusion to the questions will ideally be a shared common purpose and direction about next steps. The best of questions to your peers will be about what is success for them, what is the win-win in your respective contributions; what are the mutual dependencies and what are the ways of tackling shared risks?

Where a lengthy process is involved some of the most significant questions will be about asking for feedback from those people you most trust. When have I got it right? When have I got it abysmally wrong? Have I been learning effectively and have there been changes in my behaviour? Have I become increasingly effective or is it really time I moved on?

There are questions we ask ourselves too. What is really motivating me in this situation? Why am I spending so much time and energy on particular sub-issues? Am I getting bogged down? What really matters? What will move this issue on effectively to the next stage? What is success for me? Am I living my values effectively, have I got my balance right between my energy at work and at home? Or is dealing with this difficult issue so much sapping my energy at work that I have lost my renewable sources of energy from life outside work?

The good leader in a difficult situation is asking the right questions of themselves and of other people. There is unlikely to be a deluge of questions. The questions will be clear, thoughtful, engaging and leading to incisive discussion. The best of questions will leave people challenged and encouraged to keep going effectively. There will be no sense of an individual having been beaten up. There will have been enough space to think about the question to respond honestly and move the thinking on.

An important part of continuous learning for leaders is reflecting on what have been the most powerful questions that have made a difference in particular situations. It might have been a simple question about the next step. It might have been about what we are really trying to achieve. How will we measure success? What new approach are we going to try or how do we build ownership amongst a disparate group of people?

Questions or assertions

Does the leader gain greatest buy-in by asserting their vision and their views or by asking the questions which enable others to articulate the next steps effectively? In reality it is both rather than either of these options. But what is the right balance? Often the sign of growing confidence in a leader is that they have moved significantly from assertion to the asking of questions. They set the questions within a clear context so others know the direction of travel, but within that framework there is a focus on the use of questions to build clarity about next steps and ownership of these steps. The bright energetic leader will demonstrate their maturity as they gradually switch from assertion to question as their main means of communication.

Some personal perspectives

Charlie Massey, a board member in a national regulatory body, talks of the balance between setting direction and being clear on giving freedom. He says that one of the skills he developed as a board member was the need to give serious thought to asking the right questions. He would ask questions in different ways depending on the people he was with. Key questions for him were always:

- Can you explain to me how this fits in with our wider objectives?
- What kind of response do you need from me?

He saw this use of questions as part of a process of co-invention whereby he was enabling an individual to develop both the perspective and the tools to deal with a difficult decision well.

For May O'Keefe in her role as assistantprincipal of a sixth form college part of the attraction of using questions is that as a leader you need to be seen to be open and be seen to be taking people seriously. Her aspiration is to use an open-ended approach using questions like:

- What will happen as a result of this decision?
- What are the knock-on long-term consequences for students?
- How will this decision affect the freedom of others to make decisions?
- What will be the ripple effect throughout the whole institution?

For May, an important consideration is when to ask the key question. If an individual is in difficulties, asking a focused question at one moment can destroy their confidence completely. At another time when the question is put in a positive context then the genuine interest of the leader can help the individual lift their confidence and address the issues behind the question well and move on.

What happens when you ask a good question?

When going into a discussion where key questions need to be asked valuable elements can be:

- your dialogue within yourself before the discussion;
- the inner dialogue with others before the discussion;
- the spoken dialogue;
- the inner dialogues during the conversation;
- your reflection after the conversation; and
- the reflection of others after the conversation.

Just as you prepare for a key discussion, it may be helpful to be thinking about:

- What is the stage we have now reached?
- What are the next steps that need to happen?

- What are the key questions that will help create co-invention and constructive discussion?
- How do I set the tone so that others will be honest and open about next
steps?

While you are having this dialogue the other participants may be having a
similar dialogue covering:

- Where do we think we are in this decision-making process?
- What do we want out of the boss?
- What are the questions we want answers to?
- What sort of tone do we want the boss to set?

Part of effective preparation is not only thinking of your own questions and
what type of conclusions you want to reach; it is also about thinking about
issues others are concerned about and anticipating what their respective
questions are likely to be. Whilst the spoken dialogue happens in the meeting you may be thinking any of the following.

- Are we making good progress?
- Are my questions clear?
- Is a good debate happening?
- Are we listening to and hearing each other effectively?
- Are conclusions beginning to crystallise?

Other people in the room may be reflecting on other things.

- Is the boss fully engaged with us?
- Is there a commonality of purpose?
- Are our questions being answered?
- What is the boss saying that is giving us a useful steer?

A successful conversation about a difficult issue depends on the clarity of
the summary and about the conclusions that have been reached and agreement on the next steps. But that is not the end of the story. There will also
be questions in your mind.

- How well did I handle that discussion?
- Did the questions I asked work effectively?
- Did I leave the others feeling motivated and focused on the next steps?

The other participants in the discussion will have their own questions as well.

- Were my questions answered?
- Am I clear about next steps?
- Was I energised by that discussion?
- Has that taken us a significant step on the way to resolve key issues?

One way of developing the power of using the question is careful self-reflection after an important meeting noting down what sort of questions worked effectively both from your point of view and the point of view of other participants.

Next steps

Standing back to think through the issues to be able to ask the right questions can be an invaluable way of finding the route through to resolve difficult issues. Often, entering a meeting having reflected on the key questions is one of the most sure means of ensuring progress. Key points of reflection might be:

- How well do I use questions now?
- What can I learn from the way other people ask questions?
- In what ways might I increase my capacity to ask questions?
- Where is the right balance for me as a leader between giving directions and asking questions?

Part 3

Making difficult decisions in particular circumstances

This section of the book aims to be practical in looking at a sequence of particular situations where you are called upon to make difficult decisions. It looks at five different contexts when difficult decisions need to be made.

- As a boss.
- In relation to your boss.
- In relation to your peers.
- Dealing with your hopes and fears.
- Addressing values and priorities.

This section provides a practical set of questions addressing these specific situations. The objective is to prompt thoughts about how best to handle these sorts of situations not to provide guidance about a right answer. The prompts are set at a fairly general level so that they are applicable in a wide range of different environments. In working through each of these contexts the key questions remain.

- Do I have **clarity** in the way I am approaching this issue?
- Do I have or how can I develop a **conviction** about the right way forward and how can I test whether it is right?
- Do I have the **courage** of my convictions?
- Am I **communicating** effectively in terms of my own listening, understanding and explanation?

Chapter 10

Making difficult decisions as the boss

As the boss you might have five part-time staff working for you or you could have ten thousand people within your area of responsibility spread globally. The boss is often in an exposed, lonely position. Everyone they turn to for advice may have a vested interest and therefore temper their comments. Perhaps the best preparation for you as a leader in making difficult decisions is:

- be **clear** about what you are expected to deliver and what you want to achieve;
- have **conviction** and passion in the way you lead your people;
- have the **courage** to take individuals forward into new situations;
- be conscious of – and confident in – your **communication** role.

This chapter looks at five different types of situations, namely:

- introducing better decision-making into your senior team;
- changing the values of your organisation;
- taking a decision when your senior team have differing views;
- moving a senior member out of your team; and
- being compelled to readdress an issue.

Introducing better decision-making into your senior team

The need to introduce better decision-making may result from: your observations arriving newly into the role, the feedback from members of the team, the views of customers and external stakeholders, the results of external reviews, or the consequences of decisions that have not gone well.

Practical steps that might be worth considering could include:

- invite the team to analyse what has worked well or less well in a dispassionate way;
- use external facilitation to help crystallise the evidence of success or failure;
- invite team members to describe what good decision-making would look like and what needs to be in place for that type of decision-making to happen effectively;
- observe other teams to see what works well for them and what lessons might be transferable;
- seek the views of non-executives on the decision-making process, inviting them to provide objective and focused feedback;

- encourage a junior colleague to sit in on team discussions and then express views afterwards on what they thought worked well or less well;
- share experiences with members of other teams, perhaps observing them in operation;
- work hard at reaching agreement about the appropriate decision-making processes for the future and test the approach out in an initial meeting or two;
- put in place an external review of these processes after, say, six months;
- ensure there is a strong discipline about the way items are introduced at the start of a discussion;
- ensure clarity in the way conclusions are stated and recorded; and
- be clear in advance what success is in terms of the type of decisions made, and then review progress on the decisions after a year.

Changing the values of your organisation

A good moment to observe objectively the values of an organisation is when you first arrive in a role, as the clarity of your perspective will steadily diminish over time. It is grasping the moment to fully understand what are the values you are observing, what are your own values and how do the two interrelate. After you have been in an organisation for a while it is the perspective of an external observer that can be so valuable in highlighting the extent to which values are being lived.

Key steps in changing the values of an organisation might be:

- be clear what your own values are and what are the behaviours that flow from those values;
- invite others to express what for them are the most important values and what are the resulting behaviours that matter most to them;
- use staff surveys or 360° feedback approaches to elicit views on how others in the organisation see the values being lived;
- use external consultants to interview a cross section of individuals and describe the values as perceived and lived;
- consider systematically your personal values and how they relate to the organisational values, being conscious whether they are consistent or contradictory with each other;
- define clearly for the future what are the values that are most important for the organisation and do this wherever possibly jointly with your team followed by wide consultation;
- ensure that once you have defined the organisational values, that you and your senior team are explicit about them and live them;

- allow people to challenge you if you and your team are not living their values;
- be clear what behaviours in an organisation should stop and adopt a zero tolerance approach if they continue; and
- celebrate living the values as they impact on the organisation.

Taking a decision when your senior team have differing views

Living in a situation where members of a senior team have different views can be an expression of success. Where a leader appoints 'clones' to their team and there is limited disagreement the discussions are unlikely to be creative. The price of creating a team whose members have a variety of perspectives is that markedly differing views might be expressed.

Taking a decision when there are differing views among a team might involve the following actions:

- listen carefully to the views of each team member and demonstrate that you are listening carefully;
- get to the bottom of their views and put in the intellectual and emotional energy to do this;
- ensure there is a good quality of dialogue between team members that is reflective and creative, and avoids shouting from the trenches;
- ensure that the discussions put the decision into an appropriate context about the need for this decision and the constraints upon it;
- invite participants to be very clear what they think and why, and be willing to be open to changing their ideas;
- be ready to encourage trade-offs between different sets of decisions where this does not undermine the integrity of each decision;
- recognise when you have 'capital in the bank' and can afford to make a decision even though you do not have consensus knowing that the members of the team will back you;
- explain your reasons carefully at each stage and never get emotionally rattled with your colleagues;
- as you become clearer in your view be explicit about your conclusions while allowing people time to get used to your conclusions;
- flag up what your likely decision is going to be and when you are going to make it, so that there is one – and only one – final opportunity for colleagues to try to influence your conclusion; and
- be available to talk through the conclusion one-to-one so that individuals can get fully used to it and feel that they have understood your perspective.

- Put in place review points to assess whether a decision is working at an appropriate time afterwards (e.g. six months).
- Do not rush the process of decision-making, but then be clear when a decision has been taken.
- Be very explicit about what the decision is, both orally and in writing, and ensure it is communicated effectively.

Moving a senior member out of your team

This can be one of the most important and sensitive decisions that any leader makes. When asked about the toughest decision that he had made in his first five years as Permanent Secretary at the UK Department for International Development Suma Chakrabarti said,

> *'Giving early retirement to one of my very senior colleagues whose performance had waned. It was a colleague I admired a lot so, emotionally, it was a very tough decision to make. He was my mentor in many ways, always my colleague and a friend. Gearing myself up to make the decision and then taking him through it was very hard.'*

Suma talks of developing a stock of emotional resilience to make these types of decisions. Moving on a senior member of your team can be one of the most emotionally draining decisions, particularly when there has been a history of working effectively as colleagues together. Often the decision, although initially painful, turns out best for both the individual and the organisation. The frequent response from both parties involved in this sort of decision is often that the change could with advantage have been made earlier.

Key considerations when moving on a senior member of your team might be:

- be very clear about your reasons;
- do not to make a decision in haste but reflect on it carefully before actioning it;
- triangulate your reactions with those who you trust who come from different perspectives;
- ensure there is clarity in your mind about what the individual has done well in the past. This will be a cross check to try to understand why things are not going as well now and provide a basis for a positive set of explanations for the individual and for use with colleagues and more widely;

- try to sit inside the shoes of the team member so you understand how they are likely to react and what is going to work best for them in terms of moving on smoothly;
- encourage an individual to focus on what they might want to be doing next and see if progress can be made using this approach before there is any suggestion of pressing the individual to move;
- be clear about the reasons for the need for a change using dispassionate arguments wherever possible about the changing context together with positive arguments about how the individual's strengths might be better suited in other roles;
- prepare the way with the individual through more than one discussion and never put an item about an individual's personal future at the tail end of a business meeting with a tight time constraint;
- give the individual personal space to reflect on your view and do not bounce them, whilst giving a clear timetable;
- ensure the individual has heard the message and is not in denial of receipt of the message;
- allow the individual to announce their own next steps wherever possible;
- celebrate their contribution and allow the individual to move on with honour;
- be unambiguous in terms of the need for change if the individual continues to be resistant, and illustrate a willingness to be explicit publicly if they are showing a reluctance to move on in a constructive way;
- ensure as far as possible that the working relationship ends on good terms with an agreed way of keeping in touch where you wish to do so;
- recognise throughout this process that you are wanting to create a future ally and not someone who will happily 'knife you in the back'.

Being compelled to readdress an issue

You may have set a clear course and made a decision based on the best evidence available. You may have spent hours persuading people this is the right course of action. You have invested a great deal of your personal capital and energy, and built a strong support for your action.

But then an external factor hits you. The stock market falls, or prices for your product drop, or new data comes to light, or a merger changes everything. You feel stranded and lost. Your effort has been wasted. You fear your people will question your wisdom and foresight. You suspect your colleagues may be secretly celebrating your misfortune.

So what do you do? The first inclination may be to have a tantrum, or go away to hide. You know you cannot ignore the problem and just to worry about it is not helping at all. So what next? Some possible next steps might include:

- stand back and assess how significant the changed circumstances are;
- identify what your emotional reaction is and try to separate that out from your assessment of the facts;
- talk to a trusted friend so you are able to get your reaction into perspective;
- think through the reasons for your original decision and consider whether the new circumstances are significant enough to influence the original decision;
- look again at the original objectives. Are they still valid?
- reflect on what is now the right mix of next steps to be considering;
- talk through their reactions with those who may be most concerned by the new external factors; and finally
- consider how you can best regroup the team involved so that they can be re-energised to look at next steps in a positive way.

If part of the problem is that you made a hasty decision originally that increased future risks, be ready to admit your culpability and say how you want to take forward next steps and learn from what happened in the past. You will need to acknowledge openly why you have readdressed an issue, what your learning has been and how you want to ensure the revised objectives are met.

Next steps

In these five types of situations as a leader there could be a regular returning to the 4Cs:

- **clarity:** am I clear in my own mind and am I bringing enough clarity in the way I am explaining my perspective?
- **conviction:** am I measuring my approach against my values and am I believing in what I am doing in a way that is based on experience, my values and reality?
- **courage:** am I demonstrating both the courage to act and the courage to listen to others?
- **communication:** am I balancing effectively listening and explaining? Am I getting enough feedback about how well I am managing the process and the outcomes?

Chapter 11

Making difficult decisions in relation to your boss

One of the most important skills to develop is effective upward manage-ment. You may have strong views on the way the boss works, but at the end of the day the boss is the boss. The boss will always be open to influence from someone they trust, even though the degree of influence may some-times appear marginal.

Key elements of effective upward management include:

- **clarity** about respective roles;
- **conviction** about the best of way of influencing someone;
- **courage** to be clear in your views and not be overawed by an individual's status; and
- effective **communication** with the boss both formally and informally.

It is always worth remembering that the person who is currently your boss will not always be your boss. He or she will move on and be able to influ-ence your future elsewhere, sometimes you might eventually become the individual's boss. Once you have built up a trusted relationship it can turn into a mentoring relationship or a professional friendship.

This chapter addresses the following areas:

- enabling your boss to face up to a decision they are ducking;
- influencing your boss to make a decision in support of your favoured ap-proach;
- holding firm when your boss is demanding an immediate decision; and
- rebuilding the relationship after a difference of view on a decision.

Enabling your boss to face up to a decision they are ducking

All of us put some decisions into the 'too difficult' category. Or perhaps it is a minor decision that we never get round to looking at until it becomes a difficult decision! Sometimes we park decisions because we do not have the information or the time or the emotional energy to deal with them. Some-times we are very conscious of this parking of decisions while on other occasions we almost blind ourselves to the fact that we have taken such an action. We are then dependent on a colleague pointing out that a decision really does need to be taken.

Enabling your boss to face up to a decision they are ducking is not straightforward. But it can often be the most useful type of reminder that a colleague can make. Key steps in this can be:

- build a track record of loyalty to your boss in taking forward previous decisions;
- develop the type of relationship with your boss which is based on trust which enables both of you to speak openly about aspects that are going well or less well;
- grow a pattern of giving feedback when invited to do so or when a suitable opportunity arises, so that the boss is used to a pattern of thoughtful and sensitive feedback;
- get into a pattern of asking questions about what might be happening next on particular issues (including an issue that the boss is ducking);
- refer to the benefits which will flow when a decision has been made on a particular issue;
- ask how you can help in resolving a particular difficult issue;
- invite the boss to say at what point it will be possible to make a decision on a subject;
- encourage the boss to take time out in order to reach a decision;
- demonstrate your commitment to take forward the decision when it has been reached;
- sometimes show controlled irritation when no decision has been taken while being careful to ensure that such action is not counterproductive.

Influencing your boss to make a decision in support of your favoured approach

Influencing your boss to make a decision in support of your favoured approach might in some people's eyes, be regarded as manipulation. The aim, however, is to put a set of arguments in such a way that they are convincing. If the boss is convinced other people are likely to be persuaded too. Influencing a boss effectively to make a decision in support of your favoured approach almost invariably involves being open-minded so that your favoured approach evolves in the light of the feedback from the boss.

Key elements can include:

- involve the boss from an early stage in the thinking so that they can influence the initial shape of the likely decision;
- allow your boss to steer you in your thinking on matters that enable your favoured approach to be delivered effectively without fundamentally altering your favoured approach;
- always be clear about what you see as the benefits of your favoured approach;

- be open about the negatives of your favoured approach with measured explanations of why the downsides are not significant;
- be unwaveringly positive about the boss's contribution but never do so in an ingratiating or artificial way;
- link the outcomes of your favoured approach to the overall outcomes that the organisation is seeking to attain;
- build champions in support of your approach who can influence the boss;
- be very careful about creating a situation where your boss feels that he is being 'boxed in' to a particular conclusion;
- give the boss the discretion to make decisions on certain elements;
- celebrate the contribution and guidance of the boss;
- discreetly remind people from time to time of the benefits that flowed from the decision to support your favoured approach.

Holding firm when your boss is demanding an immediate decision

Giving yourself space can be so important when the boss is seeking an immediate decision. The space you need may not be a long time, it might be half-an-hour's break or five minutes reflection. It might mean sleeping on an issue overnight and giving a firm decision in the morning.

In a world that is moving ever faster the need to make instant decisions seems to become relentlessly stronger. The pace of information exchange seems to legitimise bosses demanding immediate responses which can be counterproductive. So what happens when you are put under pressure to make an immediate decision? Some of the ways of handling that situation might include:

- be determined to keep your cool;
- create the time to think, be it for five minutes or an hour;
- be as clear as possible in your own mind what the reasons are for an immediate decision;
- briefly imagine or write down the consequences of the alternative approaches;
- create a reason to delay a decision overnight if that is possible;
- speak to one or two significant others to get a perspective from trusted, knowledgeable and independent people;
- do something physical - it might just be walking around the room, or it might be a brisk lunchtime walk or an evening visit to the gym;

- think for a focused period about something completely different that will take you into another world and help put the decision into a wider perspective: your thoughts might focus on your family, your travels or the last weekend;
- accept the need for an early decision and stop fighting it when it becomes clear that an early decision is unavoidable: it is moving on emotionally from a sense of resentment or panic into a calm acceptance that a decision has to be taken;
- reflect on what your values tell you, possibly pondering on what impact particular organisational or personal values have on this decision;
- remember to mark the moment when you have made this decision through acknowledging to yourself that you have made a tough decision and allowing yourself to feel satisfied that you have been able to do so.

Rebuilding a relationship after a difference of view on a decision

The aftermath following a difference of view on a decision has to be handled carefully. If there have been heated or emotive exchanges, it may take a while to restore the relationship. But it can be even more difficult where individuals come out of a decision-making process feeling inwardly resentful or cross. Rebuilding relationships carefully is essential for the future smooth running in any organisation.

Key elements of rebuilding relationships might include:

- leave a cooling off period but not one that extends too long;
- remember that your own emotions may well be mirrored by the other person: if you are feeling cross they are quite likely to be cross too;
- be positive about the contribution of the boss on other issues, saying this in meetings or e-mails and looking like you mean it;
- ensure there are positive discussions with the boss on other topics and make clear how much you appreciate their contribution on these topics;
- invite your boss informally into a different context, possibly for coffee, a drink or for lunch;
- say so if you think you got your approach wrong and build a reputation for openness and a willingness to learn;
- invite your boss to talk through the decision with you in an informal setting in order to find a new way forward;
- show yourself ready to move on to other topics;

- demonstrate that you hold no grudges; but
- watch your back to ensure that no one takes advantage of the fact that there had been a marked difference of view between yourself and your boss.

Next steps

Working effectively with your boss will always involve careful thought and planning and thinking through how best to upwardly manage them. Doing this effectively is no sinecure but where an individual builds up a significant level of trust with their boss then the team becomes more than the sum of the parts through the strengthening of each others' ability to make difficult decisions well.

It can be worth reflecting using the 4Cs:

- **clarity:** has the relationship with the boss become better or worse over recent months?
- **conviction:** have I moved the relationship on in a way which is consistent with my values and those of the boss?
- **courage:** have I been bold enough in expressing my views?
- **communication:** is there an increased level of understanding between you and your boss? Has the communication worked effectively?

Chapter 12

Making difficult decisions in relation to your peers

Often, the experience in decision-making is that the building up of and use of allies is so important in ensuring success. Building support among peers may seem an irrelevant investment in the short term. But taking a wider view about what success is will often mean building and maintaining the support of key colleagues and networks.

The key strands can be:

- **clarity:** being clear who the peers are who can ensure the success of your plans or put the kibosh on them;
- **conviction:** being determined to work closely with your peers and not ignore them;
- **courage**: putting in the energy to build support from others and not assuming that success just results from winning the intellectual argument; and
- **communication:** using a variety of means to maintain and enhance constructive relationships with a range of peers.

This chapter addresses the following:

- persuading a peer that the decision they are moving towards is wrong;
- building support from colleagues for a decision you want to make;
- building a relationship with peers which provides a framework for effective future decision-making ; and
- building a wider network that will enable decisions to be made more effectively in the future.

Persuading a peer that the decision they are moving towards is wrong

Sometimes you observe a peer who is fixated on a particular approach: they seem blind to the wider context and the influence of others. What is the best way of influencing someone in that situation? Key steps might be:

- ensure the day-to-day relationship is warm, courteous and constructive;
- be supportive in practical ways in helping the individual address other issues they are facing;
- agree explicitly with other decisions the individual is making and ensure they know you agree with them;

- seek an opportunity for a private one-to-one discussion in an informal environment where you can express your concerns and show you are listening hard;
- set out your concerns and suggest a way forward clearly but in a reflective way with careful acknowledgement of the reasons why the peer is taking the view they are;
- encourage the peer to think through different angles and seek an opportunity to continue the discussion at a later date;
- be explicit about the evidence and strength of support for your favoured view;
- build alliances with others and draw attention to these alliances;
- appeal to a shared set of values;
- refer discreetly to past occasions when your perspective has proved right;
- if the peer does change their view allow them to present it as a result of their own thinking;
- never overly express personal pride about persuading somebody to change their mind.

Building support from colleagues for a decision you want to make

You may have been focusing on a particular issue for some time. You are clear about the preferred way ahead but know that you must build support before your preferred option will become the agreed way forward.

Key elements are:

- ensure the day-to-day relationship with your peers is constructive and warm;
- show continued support for your colleagues in their areas of primary concern;
- seek their views at a formative stage listening hard to their perspective and concerns;
- try to reflect some of their concerns in your next steps;
- give your colleagues explicit credit for their contribution and influence;
- try to identify the win-win situation where the consequence of your getting agreement to your approach also means benefits for others;
- share your proposals at an interim stage which allows them to be shaped by others;
- be explicit about the evidence and value basis for the decision;

- seek explicit help from colleagues in carrying forward the outcomes of the decision;
- publicly knowledge the contribution of your colleagues.

Building a relationship with peers which provides the framework for effective future decision-making

Long-term investment in relationships can prove invaluable when it comes to future decision-making. In most of my career within the UK Government Civil Service there was not a great deal of contact between people from different departments although I was privileged to work in five departments and so built up a network of friends and colleagues. Recent initiatives such as the High Potential Development Scheme have brought together high potential individuals from a range of different departments into a variety of learning situations. The friendship bond between these individuals is now strong. They will create a much more collegiate senior cadre than has previously existed. Their ability to make difficult decisions co-operatively when different departmental interests are at stake will be much greater than for previous generations.

So, what are the key ingredients in building a future capability in decision-making by senior groups and teams? Elements include:

- build and encourage networks at junior levels;
- encourage individuals to be open about their strengths and areas for development;
- create team exercises which take people outside their comfort zones and enable them to experiment with different approaches;
- encourage individuals to be open to feedback both positive and developmental;
- encourage individuals to move through a variety of roles so that they are part of a variety of teams over a period of time;
- encourage individuals to be part of teams in other spheres (e.g. in a voluntary capacity in the local community) and to draw lessons from their experiences of working in a variety of different teams;
- encourage individuals to be committed to each other's success and to measure success not by their own attainment but by the outcomes of particular organisations of which they are part;
- reward teams that include people who come together from different spheres and have demonstrated the capability quickly to work well together; and

- encourage individuals to maintain links with colleagues with whom they have worked well in the past through continuing encouraging and mentoring each other.

Building a wider network which will enable decisions to be made more effectively in the future

The focus is often on influential peers within the organisation in which you currently work. But success will often be dependent upon the support of stakeholders from a much wider network. Building up contacts and alliances with people across a wider network can produce allies who can play a part in future decision-making .

Key questions in building a wider network might include:

- how much time and energy do i want to invest in creating a wider network?
- who are the people with whom there is a shared set of values and interest?
- who stimulates my thinking and with whom is there creative discussion?
- where is there a commonality of interest which it is worth developing?
- what are my necessary areas of learning and how will talking to particular individuals help my own learning?
- what are the win-win situations i can help create where there is a strong mutuality of learning and understanding?
- how best can i build networks (e.g. via e-mail, learning sets, informal lunches, or one-to-one discussions);
- how do i best keep informal contacts fresh and creative?
- who can i sensibly introduce to other colleagues where the networking is likely to be based on shared values and mutual understanding?
- what am I learning about my own decision-making processes from talking with individuals in a wide range of spheres: can I keep developing this thinking through continued contact and understanding?

Next steps

The whole area of building relationships and common interests with peers is often neglected. But building their support and taking account of their wisdom is an essential part of building credibility as a decision maker who can operate on a significant stage. Questions to ask yourself about next steps might be based on the 4Cs.

- **clarity:** which three peers do I want to build a strengthened relationship with?
- **conviction:** which of my peers am I nervous about and how can I build a better relationship with them?
- **courage:** which peers give me courage and which dissipate my courage? What do I take from that experience?
- **communication:** what is the step change I need to take in communicating with my peers?

Chapter 13

Dealing with your hopes and fears

The effective leader may look to be gliding effortlessly while peddling furiously below the surface. Creating success is rarely a smooth, calm operation. There is often a plethora of hopes and fears which are an essential part of making progress. The hopes create the drive for change while fears can be terrible inhibitors but also powerful drivers to make a difference.

In Chapter 4 on courage we looked at ways of handling and overcoming fears. This chapter looks at specific types of situations when we can be gripped by fear. What can help is an approach based on the 4Cs.

- **clarity:** being as objective as possible about our own hopes and fears and trying to address them constructively.
- **conviction:** developing enough self-belief to cope with our fears and use them to good effect.
- **courage:** accepting that sometimes we have to 'grit our teeth' and decide.
- **communication:** recognising that we rarely act alone with a continuous focus on listening and talking being essential.

The chapter specifically addresses:

- handling a situation where you are indecisive;
- facing a decision you do not like taking;
- recovering from a wrong decision; and
- holding firm when courage fails you.

Handling a situation where you are indecisive

Being gripped by indecision is not something that you alone have experienced. Most leaders go through periods of doubt when they find it difficult to make up their minds on a particular issue. Possible approaches to help address this might be:

- write down the pros and cons about a particular decision;
- imagine you have made a particular choice and see what your reactions are to that choice;
- make a decision in your mind, put it on one side and see whether in a day or two you are content with that 'decision' or are distinctly uneasy about it;
- reflect on what works for you in terms of the rhythm of making decisions and see whether this decision can be fitted into that rhythm;

- reflect on previous moments of indecision and what has helped you come out of them;
- accept that for a period you are going to be indecisive about a particular issue and park that issue but give yourself a time frame for when you will return to it;
- observe how other people have coped with periods of indecision and ask them what their learning has been from these times;
- consider what reward you will give yourself when you have made the decision (the reward can be quite minor and need not involve significant expenditure!);
- let your mind go blank and dream and see if in the empty space you begin to see the decision through a different perspective;
- begin to articulate the benefits of having made a decision;
- talk through the potential benefits of a decision with different people;
- use a discussion with a mentor or coach to help you crystallise next steps; and
- begin to articulate some of the damage that will be done if no decision is taken.

Facing a decision you do not like taking

Some decisions just stay on the edge of the desk. We want them to fall into the wastepaper bin, but they still sit there becoming curled at the edges. We may not want to take a particular decision because of its repercussions, it may be emotionally difficult, or similar decisions have proved painful before.

How might we best get ourselves into a situation where we are prepared to face a decision we do not like taking? Possible ways forward are:

- reflect on what time of day or time of week you are best able to take difficult decisions;
- imagine the positive effects of taking a decision and how that will enable progress to be made in different areas;
- imagine the consequences of not taking a decision and the potential damage that will be done;
- be as clear as you can about why you do not like making this decision and define how much of that is rational and how much is emotional;
- talk through the decision with significant others, maybe a friend who has helped you work through decisions you did not like taking before;

- reflect on how you have coped with other decisions in the past that you have not liked taking, and consider what has worked for you in moving the decision on;
- possibly shift your mind completely into making a decision in an area that is more comfortable to you: once you have the pleasure of success in being able to make a decision in that area revert to the decision which you are not finding it easy to take;
- reflect on whether your difficulty in taking a decision in this area does have implications: do you need some further training or is it time you moved to a different area of work?
- define as clearly as you can what is getting in the way and how you can move or get round that impediment;
- reflect on the reward you will give yourself when you have taken the decision that you do not want to take; and
- reflect on your personal values or beliefs that are relevant for this decision, this might help you overcome your indecision.

Recovering from a wrong decision

An individual who has never made a wrong decision is either arrogant or blind to the impact of their own actions. Our lives are littered with wrong decisions. In one sense there is no such thing as a wrong decision. It is a matter of ensuring that you gain effective learning from all the decisions you make.

Norman Haste with his extensive experience of leading major infrastructure projects talks of responding to major engineering failures. He comments,

> 'When there has a major engineering failure it has rarely been caused by a single reason. It has been a combination of events. You have to grin and bear it and sort it out. There has to be lots of support for the people involved. When things go wrong you work with the people who know the conditions best and watch out for the risks of going for an external solution. You put in a recovery plan after carefully looking at the risks. You put things right first and do the inquest later.'

When you as an individual recognise that you have made a wrong decision and need to move on the following might be helpful:

- admit you made a mistake and don't try to cover it up;
- stop digging holes for yourself by making the situation worse: i.e. don't keep trying to persuade yourself that a wrong decision was a right decision;
- be clear what your learning has been through this experience;
- demonstrate through your words and actions that you have learnt your lesson from this experience;
- be conscious of the audit trial: be explicit as to why you made the particular decision and the considerations you were taking into account;
- regard every experience of a decision that has gone wrong as an invaluable part of your life;
- be ready to position yourself differently on the next decision of a similar nature so you do not fall into the same trap again;
- ask others how they have moved on after they have taken wrong decisions;
- allow yourself to be encouraged by the experience of others;
- accept that some will blame you and that that level of blame will stay with them for a long time: accept that you may be able to move on more easily than others;
- if the wrong decision has had negative consequences be ready to accept that it might be right for you to move on to another sphere of work: try to regard that as an invaluable learning experience and not as a failure; and
- try to draw a line under the event in your mind so that it does not become a recurring nightmare.

Holding firm when courage fails you

There are times when our supporters seem to drift away. Our courage begins to sag and we start wondering whether we have been set up to fail. Norman Haste tells of a time when he started to lose faith in his own conviction during a trades' union dispute. He said that the management needed to stick out for three months but his colleagues were only prepared to go along with his view for two weeks. He had to decide whether to continue to resist the union demands. He said,

> 'I had to make a decision when unsure about the consequences. It came down to a sense of leadership and conviction. I felt I was right even though there was a nagging uncertainty. I had never before been under so much pressure to take a different approach. I felt very isolated. I just held on to my conviction that we were doing the right thing. After 10

days the Unions returned asking for their jobs back on the same terms and conditions. I had been vindicated and had come through a difficult period of isolation.'

Holding firm when going through a bleak period might be helped by the following:

- be clear in your own mind why you have made a particular decision;
- keep your eyes fixed on the ultimate goal whatever the hesitancy from others;
- hold on to good things in your life in parallel worlds so your life is not completely dominated by this one issue;
- see and enjoy good friends and ensure there is plenty of laughter;
- remember there are various phases to life accepting that some are more tortuous than others;
- imagine there is light at the end of the tunnel and what that would look like;
- keep up the physical exercise and the sense of physical vitality;
- hold on to the personal beliefs that are most important to you as you work through a bleak period;
- try to stand back and see the situation as objectively as you can;
- enjoy doing something completely different that might give you energy and will feed back into dealing with this difficult situation; and
- focus on the personal learning and strength that flows from dealing with this type of situation effectively.

Next steps

The learning that comes from these types of difficult decisions when our fears get in the way can be about:

- **clarity**: a much better understanding of ourselves;
- **conviction**: a recognition of the importance of our beliefs and values in taking us difficult decision-making periods;
- **courage**: a recognition that perhaps we have more courage than sometimes we recognise in ourselves; and
- **communication**: the importance of keeping talking with ourselves so that we do not let ourselves be strangled by the grip of fear or failure.

Chapter 14

Addressing values and priorities

We are not machines making impersonal decisions. Our values and those of the organisations within which we work impact on the way we make decisions and on priorities. Any healthy organisation is mindful of the behaviours operating within the organisation and is regularly reviewing the values that it wants to encourage. The healthy organisation recognises that individuals are themselves made up of various beliefs and values and are not just intellectual or emotional beings. They work best when they have a strong sense of purpose and feel valued for their contribution. When there is that resonance between the individual's contribution and the needs and hopes of the organisation there is the greatest chance of success and personal fulfilment.

The relevant context for this chapter is:

- **clarity:** the importance of recognising that values and beliefs are key drivers;
- **conviction:** acknowledging that the resonance between individual and corporate values can be a powerful motivator for success;
- **courage:** the value of encouraging people to work through issues explicitly and not regarding them as irrelevant;
- **communication:** the importance of listening, and recognising how the actions of individual leaders impact on the whole organisation because of the intense way in which they are observed.

This chapter looks in turn at the following situations:

- guarding against difficult decisions sapping energy;
- work and personal priorities are at odds with each other;
- work and personal values are at odds with each other; and
- balancing long- and short-term personal priorities.

Guarding against difficult decisions sapping energy

Taking demanding decisions can be both exhilarating and exhausting with the two processes often happening at the same time. The issue is whether the exhaustion is temporary tiredness or a debilitating form of exhaustion that is sapping energy away.

What might be some of the best ways of guarding against difficult decisions sapping energy? Some possible ways forward are:

- be clear on both organisational and personal values so that you are clear what, at the end of the day, is most important and how to balance potentially conflicting values;
- be clear about the sources of vitality that are most helpful to you at times when your energy is being sapped;
- set aside time for engagement in other activities in parallel worlds;
- use the approaches that work best for you in terms of switching off from work pressures;
- talk through with a coach or mentor how you handle situations where your energy is being sapped;
- spend time with friends who stimulate you and make you smile;
- reflect on what is most important in your life so that you see this decision as part of a wider context;
- be conscious of the rhythms that work best for you in terms of making decisions that tend to sap your energy; and
- recognise that when there are difficult decisions you win some and you lose some and aiming to become as philosophical as you can about decisions that are sapping your energy.

Work and personal priorities are at odds with each other

We often set ourselves a wide range of different priorities both at work and in our personal lives. The wider the range of priorities, the greater the likelihood that they will be at odds with each other. Family arrangements where both partners work make the conflict between work and personal priorities the more likely.

Some of the ways of addressing this might involve:

- be clear in your own mind what is most important to you and be explicit about this to yourself and significant others in your life;
- recognise that priorities will change but be prepared to drop priorities whenever you add new ones;
- be explicit with significant others in your life about both your personal priorities and priorities you share with them;
- be willing to be adaptable to short-term demands and not feel resentful if some personal priorities are squeezed out over the short-term;
- recognise that your priorities will change over time and therefore possibly do not tie yourself too rigidly to one immediate set of priorities;

- always test your personal priorities against your beliefs and values to reduce the likelihood of discontinuity between personal values, personal priorities and work objectives;
- be honest with yourself about the drivers that are most important to you at work;
- be honest with yourself about the role that ambition has in driving you to success;
- be clear in your own mind about where finance fits in so personal financial aspiration is consciously prioritised within your life plan so you are 'building up treasure' in the place that is most important to you;
- be clear to yourself about the consequences of your actions on others; and
- be conscious that even if the quantity of time you are able to spend with people is limited, that the quality of that time is high.

Work and personal values are at odds with each other

Contexts where work and personal values are at odds may well be different to situations where work and personal priorities are at odds. Addressing work and personal priorities may just be a matter of time and energy, while addressing work and personal values when they are at odds may need more fundamental review.

Addressing a situation where work and personal values are at odds can lead to the need to switch activities or jobs completely. It can result in a fundamental reappraisal of next steps. Possible ways to address this might include:

- reassess the personal values that are most important to you;
- put those values into a hierarchy of relative importance;
- be explicit to yourself about where there is room for compromise and where there is no room for compromise;
- be explicit with yourself about how important work is and how tied you are to this particular type of work and organisation you are currently engaged with;
- consider which values of the organisation you most resonate with and reflect on how you can build on those;
- be clear in your own mind about what values you have difficulty with at work and how you want to address that difficulty;
- reflect on who you can talk these issues through with outside the organisation to help clarify your thinking;

- push the door to see if it is possible to have an open discussion with your boss about these concerns;
- be clear about what your sticking points are and where you can be flexible; and
- think hard about how you want to resolve the situation either by staying within the organisation or moving on.

Balancing long- and short-term priorities

Because we live in a busy world we tend to be focused in the current moment with present priorities becoming all-consuming. There are times when we are catapulted into thinking about long-term priorities when there is illness or bereavement. There might be moments of personal reflection on holiday or at significant festivals when we do think about the longer term, but so often we return to daily business and pressures quickly.

Possible ways of addressing the dilemma between long- and short-term priorities might include:

- be explicit about what is important to you now;
- reflect on how your priorities are beginning to change;
- write down what might be your most important priorities in five years time;
- consider the extent to which your short-term priorities influence your desired long-term outcomes;
- be honest about how your values are influencing your priorities;
- recognise what the balance is between your priorities and your physical capability and energy, and how you see that changing;
- be honest about the match between your priorities and your rational and emotional capabilities;
- consider the personal development and learning you need to engage in to get your priorities more in line with each other; and
- ensure there is clarity in your mind about what personal fulfilment is and how, looking back from a future date, you would want to describe the way you balanced your different priorities.

Next steps

Addressing values and priorities is fundamental to getting into a position where difficult decisions can be put into perspective and handled well. Some of the next steps might be.

- **clarity:** recognising the reality of the extent to which your values and priorities are in harmony or not;
- **conviction:** accepting the importance of the way your values influence the way you make decisions;
- **courage:** being ready to make tough decisions about your own priorities; and
- **communication:** always keeping the engagement working effectively at a personal level with those most important to you.

Chapter 15

Next steps

A former junior fire officer tells the story of going into a building to try and find two children. He was told he had 90 seconds before the building was likely to collapse. He rushed up the stairs and had to make the decision whether to go into the room on the right or the left, as there was only time to investigate one room. He had to make an instant decision. It happened to be the wrong one: the children must have been in the other room. He now had to exit the building in the time allowed or he would have lost his own life.

This experience has lived with this former junior fire officer for a long time. His only choice was an instant decision: he assumed the children were in the bedroom, when they must have moved into the lounge. The story could either have been a continuing source of personal anguish or an example of the importance of making decisions recognising that some of them will be wrong. The worst choice would have been for the junior fire officer to stand on the landing weighing up which decision to take while precious seconds slipped away.

Some decisions have to be instant while others need to take time and careful thought. For example, a decision to bar an individual from working with children involves rigorous examination of the evidence. Often the decision is clear when legal convictions mean there is only one proper decision, but sometimes only limited information is available. In these situations a decision whether or not to ban somebody from working with young people is a matter of judgement requiring clear thinking without a rushed conclusion.

Set alongside these examples concerned with life and death and children's safety, many of the decisions we take pale into relative insignificance. We owe a debt to those willing to take these hard decisions that protect our health and well being.

My hope for you is that having read this book you will be more attuned to the decisions you need to make, more aware of the experience of others and better equipped to make the decisions ahead of you. You will see the decisions you make in a wider perspective and have an accurate view about their relative degree of difficulty.

Decision-making is unlikely to come easily to you, and nor should it. If decisions are too easy we are unlikely to be seeing the effects on others or appreciate the ultimate consequences of our decisions. But we can take practical steps to improve our ability to make difficult decisions. Applying the 4Cs of **clarity, conviction, courage** and **communication** can equip us to move on by enabling us to:

- be clearer about key aspects of the issues, context and consequences;
- apply our intuition, values, experience and trained judgement to best effect;
- turn our belief into action to ensure effective next steps; and
- use a wide range of communication approaches to listen, understand, engage and persuade.

We can improve our ability to make difficult decisions by observing others and drawing on experiences from each area of our lives. Our experience from our family, community, sport, hobby or faith worlds can reinforce our sensitivities and capabilities in making difficult decisions at work. Being decisive about personal priorities can improve our capacity to make decisions at work.

Some final thoughts about next steps:

- engage with the experience of those who take much more difficult decisions than you;
- look for the personal release and acceptance which comes from taking difficult decisions thoughtfully;
- let your values influence your decisions so you favour the best answer and not the easy answer;
- school yourself in embedding the ability to make difficult decisions well; and
- draw on the support and stretch from colleagues, trusted friends and a mentor or coach but ensure you are your own person and are not unreasonably influenced by the views of others.

Making difficult decisions is both a responsibility and a privilege. So put fear or apprehension to one side and make those difficult decisions that need to be made.

Selected bibliography

Baden-Fuller, Charles, (2003), 'Strategic Decision Making in Large Complex Organisations;, London: *Risk and Regulation*, Autumn edition.

Bibb, Sally and Koudi, Jeremy (2004), *Trust Matters: for organisational and personal success*, Basingstoke: Palgrove MacMillan.

Coffee, E (2003), *10 Things That Keep CEOs Awake*, London: McGraw-Hill.

Collins, J. (2001), *Good to Great*, New York: Harper.

Dawson, Heather (2007), *Thriving in a Faster Faster World*, London: Praesta.

Drucker, Peter F. (1967), 'The Effective Decision', *Harvard Business Review*, January–February edition.

Eastwood, Mairi (2007), 'Get Some Practice In', *Legal Week*, 3 May edition.

Einhorn, Hillel J. and Hogarth, Ian C, (1987), 'Decision Making: Going forward in Reverse', *Harvard Business Review*, January–February edition.

Etzioni, Amitai, (1984), 'Humble Decision Making', *Harvard Business Review*, February edition.

Goffee, R. and Jones, G., (2006), *Why Should Anyone be Lead by You?*, Boston: Harvard Business School.

Hammond, John S., Keeney, Ralph L., and Raiffa, Howard (1998) 'The Hidden Traps in Decision Making', *Harvard Business Review*, September–October edition.

Hammond, John S., Keeney, Ralph L., and Raiffa, Howard (1999), *Smart Choices: a practical guide to making better life decisions*, New York: Broadway Books.

Hayashi, Alden M., (2001), 'When to Trust your Gut', *Harvard Business Review*, February edition.

Janis, Irving and Mann, Leon (1979), *Decision Making*, Detroit: Free Press.

Martin, Roger (2007), 'How Successful Leaders Think', *Harvard Business Review*, June edition.

Mahoney, J. (1999), 'Cultivating Moral Courage in Business', in Enderle, G, ed., *International Business Ethics: Challenges and Approaches*, University of Notre Dame Press.

Paese, Matthew J. (2004), 'Executive Focus: how leaders lose it and how to regain it', *Development Dimensions International*.

Roberto, Michael, (2002), 'Making Difficult Decisions in Turbulent Times', *Ivey Business Journal*, January–February edition.

Shaw, Peter (2005), *Conversation Matters: how to engage effectively with one another*, London: Continuum.

Shaw, Peter (2006), *The Four Vs of Leadership: vision, values, value-added, vitality*, Chichester: Capstone.

Shaw, Peter (2006), *Finding your Future: the second time around*, London: Darton, Longman and Todd.

Shaw, Peter and Linnecar, Robin (2007), *Business Coaching: achieving practical results through effective engagement*, Chichester: Capstone.

Snowden, David J. and Boone, Mary E., (2007), 'A London Framework for Decision Making', *Harvard Business Review*, November edition.

Stanton Marris (2007), *Energising the Organisation Issue 10: meaningful engagement*, London: Stanton Marris.

Stewart, Bob (2006), *How to Make Decisions*, London: London Business Forum.

Index